Upper Bohemia

A MEMOIR

Hayden Herrera

SIMON & SCHUSTER

NEW YORK   LONDON   TORONTO   SYDNEY   NEW DELHI

Simon & Schuster
1230 Avenue of the Americas
New York, NY 10020

First Simon & Schuster hardcover edition June 2021

SIMON & SCHUSTER and colophon are registered trademarks of Simon & Schuster, Inc.

For information about special discounts for bulk purchases, please contact Simon & Schuster Special Sales at 1-866-506-1949 or business@simonandschuster.com.

The Simon & Schuster Speakers Bureau can bring authors to your live event. For more information or to book an event, contact the Simon & Schuster Speakers Bureau at 1-866-248-3049 or visit our website at www.simonspeakers.com.

Interior design by Carly Loman

All photos are from the collections of Hayden Herrera and Blair Resika except for page xix (bottom): photograph by Tamas Breuer, courtesy of Florence Phillips; page xxi: photograph by Joel Meyrowitz; page 10: courtesy of Peter MacMahon; page 18: courtesy of Peter Chermayeff; page 19: photograph by Sylvia Salmi, courtesy of Sophie M. Niehaus; page 38: photograph by Bertrand de Geofroy, courtesy of Nicholas Macdonald; page 55: courtesy of Daniel Potter; page 114: courtesy of Kate Manheim.

Manufactured in the United States of America

10 9 8 7 6 5 4 3 2 1

Library of Congress Cataloging-in-Publication Data has been applied for.

ISBN 978-1-9821-0528-0
ISBN 978-1-9821-0530-3 (ebook)

For Blair

Contents

Preface

O ur mother was a terrible mother, wasn't she?" My sister and I share a rueful laugh. A part of each of us wants to say, "No, she was wonderful." After a pause to search through memory, one of us nods. "Yes, she was a terrible mother." But our terrible mother gave Blair and me a wonderful life. And, she was not the only terrible mother. Most of our friends had terrible mothers, too. When we talk with friends about childhood, we compete about whose mother was the worst. This is consoling. Our mother's terribleness becomes a joke. It's not fair: our fathers are off the hook. For all his charm and wit, Blair's and mine was an absent father. As one of his wives observed, "Your father never lost a night's sleep over anybody."

My father and mother in the British Virgin Islands, 1935

In addition to their numerous love affairs, my father and mother were each married five times. They believed in the importance of pleasure, of living life to the hilt. To follow their own desire was a moral imperative. Repression, sacrifice, and compromise were cowardly. What our parents desired was not always in the best interests of their children. If they fell in love and had to pursue a new lover, they did not hesitate to stash their children with some friend, relative, or boarding school. Children were secondary to the leading of a passionate life.

What I want to understand is how could our mother have behaved the way she did? And what made the parents of our friends be impervious to their children's needs? Why did our father think it was acceptable to live in another country and to turn up now and again with a different wife? And why, if they ignored us, were Blair and I so captivated by our parents?

Our mother called her friends "upper bohemians." Most were artists or writers living in Manhattan and the Outer Cape (Wellfleet, Truro, and Provincetown) and most were born between 1908 (the year of both my parents' birth) and 1920. These so-called upper bohemians had privileged childhoods but rebelled against their parents' way of life. They rejected convention and insisted upon personal liberty. Their lives were full of adventure and drama, mixed with chaos. The flush of excitement that came with a new love affair made a marriage worn down by progeny seem dull. The sense of security and continuity, of duty fulfilled, that might have come from sticking with a spouse for the sake of the children was not enough to hold them back from the thrill of the unknown.

In a way, these upper bohemians constituted a second lost generation. They did not directly experience the horror and pointlessness of World War I, but they were affected by its aftermath, the upheaval of traditional value systems, the feeling that life is cheap and death is around the corner, so you might as well live it up. Coming of age in the late twenties, my parents absorbed that decade's disenchantment and the concomitant insistence on having fun. Unhampered by Prohibition, they were part of an alcohol culture. The cocktail hour was sacrosanct. It loosened inhibitions, allowed people to follow their impulses.

During Prohibition breaking laws became habitual. If one law could be broken, why not all? Women, who had not been welcome in saloons, joined the fray at speakeasies. Women's status changed in the 1920s. They were less submissive, more outspoken, freer to choose their own lives. For my mother and her friends, defying all norms of proper behavior was fashionable. Conformism was beneath contempt. When my mother spoke of "family values" or "togetherness" you could hear the disdain in her voice.

The Great Depression cast a pall on the madcap modes of the 1920s. When my parents' family wealth was lost or diminished after the 1929 stock market crash and after the 1932 collapse of the Swedish Match company (a Ponzi scheme controlled by Swedish

My mother, c. 1940   My father, 1948

investor, the so-called Match King, Ivar Kreuger), my father and mother had to change their way of life. They changed their world-views as well. Now nothing was permanent. Life was precarious and impecunious, but never boring. Since nothing could be taken for granted, life was an invention.

Because they were born into a world of privilege and they be-longed to what my mother called "good families" (meaning upper class), they had the gift of confidence. My parents did not have to earn confidence by achievement. Self-esteem was bestowed upon them by birth. My father, John Charles Phillips's first American ancestor, Reverend George Phillips, was educated at Cambridge University in England and came to this country in 1630 aboard the *Arbella*, the flagship of the Winthrop fleet. His descendants founded Phillips Exeter and Phillips Andover Academies.

My mother, born Elizabeth Cornell Blair, couldn't have cared less about her forebears, but she did once tell me proudly that she had Native American blood and that she was related to King John the Bad. When she had an exhibition of her paintings in Mexico City in 1949, she told a newspaper reporter that she was descended from John Paul Jones, a Scottish-born naval officer who, after killing two subordinate seamen in two separate incidents of rage, joined the Continental Navy and became a hero of the American Revolution. That her great grandfather, Ezra Cornell, founded Cornell University did not seem important enough to tell me. (Her more class-conscious younger sister made sure that Blair and I knew.)

No matter how much my parents eschewed elitism, they felt entitled. To be sure, in the 1930s, like their fellow upper bohemi-ans, they were attracted to left-wing values. They believed that all people are created equal and should have equal access to the comforts of life. My parents did not use English expressions like "Not quite out of the top drawer, dear" or "Not quite our sort, dear," for which, those in the know, say "NQOSD." Theirs was a snobbism aimed not at the lower classes or at different ethnic groups, but at the bourgeoisie and at Wall Street. No matter what your background, if you were an interesting writer or a talented painter, you could be part of "upper bohemia," a milieu that did not see a person's worth as defined by being, or not being, rich or well-born. My parents looked down on people who did not read books, look at paintings, or listen to music. My mother in particular despised vulgarity. She also loathed the "filthy rich." To her, people who had no taste were appalling. The scorn in my mother's voice when she spoke of Levittown, Howard Johnsons, billboards, Tip Top white bread, indeed anything commercialized or tacky, was chilling. She was an aesthetic fascist.

With the rise of fascism in the late 1930s and early 1940s, East Coast upper bohemia was enriched by the arrival of European émigrés. The so-called Surrealists in exile—writers like André Breton, painters like Matta Echaurren and Max Ernst—added to the intellectual and artistic effervescence. With the defeat of the Loyalists in the Spanish Civil War, the Holocaust, World War II, and the bombings of Hiroshima and Nagasaki, came a renewed sense of horror and disgust with the way people in authority ran the world. Unlike many of their upper bohemian friends who flirted with Communism, my parents' response was to turn away from political realities and to seek happiness in art and in nature.

Since they didn't have much money, they prided themselves on living hand to mouth. They and their fellow upper bohemians spurned ostentation and did their best never to look as though they had money. If they worked, it wasn't to get rich. They worked to create something—a painting, a book, a concerto, a modern house. Most of them did not have a ferocious work ethic, nor were they driven by a desire for power or fame. For them, beauty was the most important thing in the world, but if making beauty got in the way of fun, time at the easel or the writing desk could be postponed.

Perhaps my father's indifference to making money was part of his background. His father, also named John Charles Phillips and a graduate of Harvard Medical School, did not practice medicine because, he said, he didn't want to take jobs away from people who needed them. Instead he was an ornithologist, zoologist, environmentalist, and hunter who published 204 articles and books, among them the highly regarded four-volume study: *A Natural History of the Ducks.* Indeed, legend has it that the Phillips family did not come by their wealth through work. On an ocean crossing, a Bostonian Phillips met a childless English Phillips. The two men struck up a friendship and the English Phillips left his fortune to my Bostonian forebear.

My parents and their friends shared a reverence for nature that was, for some of them, a kind of religion. They were not churchgoers. They disapproved of established religions, in the case of my mother, especially Catholicism, that opium of the masses. Most were atheists. A walk in the woods, looking down at the ocean from the top of a dune, lying naked in the sun, or gazing at the night sky—that was their form of worship. They wanted to live as closely as possible to trees, ponds, fields, and the ocean. Watching birds, muskrats, and turtles was their prayer. If a great blue heron flew over the water, they were awestruck. If a human being contaminated their view, they were annoyed. A house built within their sight was an affront. Privacy was prized.

Being part of nature entailed a rather free and easy approach to sex. Married people had love affairs, and no one was shocked. Abstinence was bad for you. Frigidity was a curse. My parents agreed that sexual satisfaction was essential to happiness. Intellectual development was equally crucial. You had to expand your knowledge and develop a worldview by reading. To that end, they read D. H. Lawrence, F. Scott Fitzgerald, Henry David Thoreau, Jean-Paul Sartre, D. T. Suzuki, Edith Hamilton, Freud, and Jung. Travel was important, too. Not to know France or Italy was barbaric.

Even though they wanted a simple life, my father and mother valued sophistication. They were city people taking seasonal refuge in the country. Yet, even as they immersed themselves in European culture, they were entranced by unspoiled, indigenous "primitive" peoples, who, they thought, lived closer to elemental truths. For my mother, this belief lead to a romance with Mexico, a land she saw as not yet sullied by American vulgarity and a country where agrarian life followed age-old patterns. Reading D. H. Lawrence's *Mornings in Mexico* published in 1927 and Malcolm Lowry's *Under the Volcano* (1947) increased Mexico's allure. Mexico became a mecca, a fount of meaning and affirmation, not only for my mother (who lived there from 1948 to 1984), but also for several of her upper bohemian friends who, in the early 1950s rented houses in and around Cuernavaca. Both my parents took an increasingly dim view of the United States. To them it was a place where people lost their souls, where everyone chased after money and possessions and competed for success and fame.

My parents' haphazard approach to child rearing had much to do with their own upbringing. Reared by nannies, they saw their parents when a nanny had scrubbed them clean, dressed them nicely, and escorted them into the living room or library for a brief visit. The problem for us was that after the crash, there was no money for nannies, so we children often tagged along to adults' parties. Or were left to our own devices. These upper bohemian parents allowed their offspring a great deal of freedom. They didn't organize play dates or lessons. They did not help with homework. Their children spent many hours alone. This could be lonely, but it was beneficial. We learned to entertain ourselves. We learned to stare at the opening and closing of spaces between blades of waving grass while thinking up something to do. The child's terror of boredom could be dealt with: we had resources. We invented games, we daydreamed, we used our imaginations. Also, we had books, siblings, ponds, the ocean, and hideouts in the woods.

The Cape Cod upper bohemians had their own style. They did not wear conventional or fashionable clothing. The women preferred loose, handwoven clothes or Mexican peasant skirts and blouses. The preferred footwear was espadrilles or sandals, but going shoeless was even better. Jewelry tended to have an indigenous flavor—bold silver necklaces from Taxco, strands of heavy, pre-Columbian jade beads, or, even better, necklaces made with Native American chunks of turquoise interspersed with silver beads and animal teeth. My mother observed that artists' wives in the 1950s looked like Vikings.

In her milieu, home decoration was the opposite of what you might find in a WASP Park Avenue apartment. Our homes had no mahogany, no heavy drapes, no chintz, no chandeliers, and nothing much in the way of upholstered sofas and armchairs. My father made sofas and tables out of plywood doors to which he attached metal legs. Everyone had cheap, foldable directors' chairs with their canvas seats and backs. For a coffee table, a power company's discarded rough, wooden cable spool or a plank supported by two stacks of cinder blocks was sufficient. The kinds of houses my parents and their friends preferred were modest, light-filled, lightweight, and in harmony with nature. Since several of their friends were architects, the houses were often modern. But nothing lavish. Aesthetics were more important than comfort. A view was essential. A big kitchen or a luxurious bathroom was not. Some people had traditional Cape Cod cottages—just a couple of bedrooms and a kitchen/living room, nothing like the mansions that millionaires in fancier parts of the Cape called "cottages." My father went so far as to build what he called a "lean-to" out of cinderblock and milled wood—a permanent version of an overnight wilderness shelter.

The upper bohemians had their own style of entertaining. Food was simple. Alcohol flowed. My parents loved to give dancing parties. Since money was scarce, guests brought bottles. On Cape Cod summers, the best way to see friends was to organize a beach picnic to which people brought their own food and cooked it over a communal fire. Years later, my father bemoaned how dull and staid social life on the Cape had become. In the old days, he said, people at parties flirted purposefully and they rarely went home with the person they came with.

My parents were stars within their own community. They were talented and intelligent, but their most important asset was their

My mother, British Virgin Islands, 1935

My father, British Virgin Islands, 1935

beauty. They were so secure in their physical attractiveness that they were known to walk to a neighbor's cocktail party and mingle without clothes. My mother liked to tell me she was a "great beauty." My father was just as handsome as Gregory Peck. They did not have to make an effort to be popular. Being beautiful, like being born into the right class, gave them an unassailable self-worth. But beauty was also part of what made it possible for my mother to be such a terrible mother. Narcissism isolated her. Men loved her because she was unapproachable, the ice queen. My sister and I kept on loving her because we never stopped hoping that she would take us under her wing. Although beauty gave her power, it was, I think, a blight on her life. For her, the person that was visible from the outside did not harmonize with the person she was on the inside. She was forever restless, seeking and not finding contentment and peace.

My mother, c. 1937

My father in the 1960s

2017: View from the Porch

The wind picks up. I sit at our porch table and watch waves of light pass through lily pads and pickerel weeds as they move toward the pond's shore. One after another the ripples touch the water's edge and sink into the deep, like memories not set down. Imagining the pond's depths, alive with swaying lily pad stems, I can follow strands of time back to the beginning. The pond water is the fluid of my birth. Every time I walk into it I am born. If I stare at it, everything that happened, or most of it, will rise to the surface.

Horseleech Pond, Truro, Cape Cod

Me, Horseleech Pond, 1981

1

The Big House

When I was old enough to walk, my mother took Blair and me for afternoon swims in a place on Horseleech Pond where the reeds and lily pads parted and the sediment of dark brown leaves had been brushed aside to create a bright path of sand stretching all the way out to where the water looked dark and deep. To get to this place, my mother had cleared a trail through tupelo trees, pitch pine, and cat briar. Some parts were covered with pine needles. Other parts were blanketed with dead leaves. Under bare feet dry leaves made a nice crackle. Pine needles felt like cushions. Sunlight fell in patches on the path—light, dark, light, dark. I tried to step only on the light parts. Sometimes I had to leap. My mother pointed out wild tiger lilies and the occasional lady slipper. She told us not to pick them. If we left them, more flowers would grow next year. Following my mother single file along the narrow path, I felt like an explorer.

Blair was allowed to go over her head because she had learned to swim. She could swim out to the far side of the lily pads and poke her nose into a water lily. I was not allowed to go beyond where the water came up to my belly button. While my mother did her swift crawl out to the middle of the pond, I stood and watched a damselfly land with its luminous blue stick of a body at a right angle to a reed. Farther out much larger black dragon-flies buzzed over the water like helicopters. One of them settled on a lily pad for a moment, then flew away. We never wore bath-

Blair and me, Horseleech Pond, summer, 1941   Me, 1941

ing suits. Overhanging branches shielded us from view. Anyway, we were the only people living on Horseleech Pond. To me the place our mother took us to was secret. Only Blair and I and our mother knew how to find the path to it. Lots of people knew about our usual swimming beach where our rowboat was pulled up just downhill from our house. Our mother seemed so brave, the way she discovered new places. With her our lives were an adventure.

I had adventures that I didn't tell about. I could fly. If it was a dream, I wouldn't have known. In those days, dreams and everyday life slid into each other. I would be lying in bed and suddenly I would remember that I knew how to fly. All I had to do was breathe in and concentrate on rising. Breathe in again and I went higher. I had little control of the direction I was going in. Usually I floated in a fetal position with my face toward the sky. Sometimes I flew stretched out with my stomach facing the earth. There were times when I thought I had gone too high. I looked down at treetops and wondered if the branches would be soft if I crashed into them. But then I remembered that I could stop any fall just by taking a deep breath. I breathed in, kept floating for a while, sinking lower and lower until I found myself half asleep in bed.

My father told me how he came to own our house on Horseleech

Mother in the Big House holding Blair, 1937

Parents, Blair, and me, 1940

Pond. When he was in his last year at Harvard his great uncle by marriage, Dr. William Herbert Rollins (1852–1929) left him about eight hundred acres of land along the ocean in Wellfleet and Truro. Since Rollins and his wife, Miriam Phillips, had no children of their own, Rollins, a dentist, scientist, and inventor, took my father under his wing and taught him how to experiment and how to make things. In a May 1919 diary entry, Rollins wrote that he had helped my eight-year-old father make a pin-hole camera with which my father took and developed a photograph of rain. Rollins was also busy equipping my father with "chemicals, lanterns, scales, [and] gramme weights" for my father's upcoming solo canoe and camping trip in northern Maine. In 1930, one year after my father inherited the land, a fellow scientist wrote that, as a "lover of na-ture," Rollins had "left lands of shore and forest on Cape Cod as a sanctuary for birds." Rollins had hoped that my father would buy pieces of land in between the parcels of land bequeathed to him and eventually donate the whole thing to the Audubon, a society dedicated to conservation and to the protection of birds.

On the land that Rollins gave my father there were five sandy-bottomed kettle ponds and a long stretch of dunes and beach. Horseleech Pond, in the town of Truro, and shaped like an *8*, was the closest pond to the ocean. Around 1910, at the east end of Horseleech, in a spot separated from the ocean only by a hill that turns into a sand dune, Rollins built a 14-x-28-foot cabin, or rather he assembled it. The cabin was a Hodgson portable cottage, an early version of a pre-fab. In the second half of the 1930s, my father and mother expanded this cabin and made it their home.

My grandfather advised my father to sell the land that Rollins had given him. Bostonians did not want to go to Cape Cod, he said. There were too many black flies and mosquitos. And there were taxes, so onerous to privileged Bostonians. But the warm, almost celestial light in a painting of Horseleech Pond that my father made not long after he inherited the land, shows that he came to love this place far too much to sell it. "The atmosphere was one of complete solitude," he recalled of an early visit to the pond. "Not a soul around and we shared that little tent. And I thought, my God, if I'm really going to inherit it from my father's uncle! Well, I was impressed." In May 1930 he wrote to his mother from the camp he had just inherited: "Living conditions down here seem pretty good. Expect to stay almost indefinitely."

After graduating from Harvard in 1930, my father spent the next four years studying art, first at the Art Students League in New York, then in France, at the American Art School in Fontainebleau, and from September 1931 to May 1934 at various Parisian artists' ateliers including those of André Lhote and Fernand Léger. He married a fellow art student, Helen Schroeder, whom he described to his mother as a "swell girl . . . a blond Scandinavian type." When he returned to the United States, his marriage unraveled and early in 1935 he and Helen separated. He always told me that he already knew he didn't love Helen by the time they got married, but the wedding preparations had been so far advanced that it couldn't be stopped. He told my sister that it was a shotgun

My father skinny dipping, British Virgin Islands, 1935

wedding: Helen thought she was pregnant, but that turned out not to be the case. His letters to his mother show that the relationship was not that unhappy. It lasted some five years until his affair with his and Helen's close friend, a married woman, broke things up and his outraged parents briefly cut off his allowance.

At this point he fell in love with my mother, Elizabeth Cornell Blair. "I met Lybie at a dance at some women's club [in New York City]. . . . We danced together a good bit; but nothing happened after that. Later, during a long, grim winter, I met her at the 86th Street subway station—she asked me up for a drink, then one thing led to another." At that time, my mother was unhappily married to John Potter, a handsome athletic young man who owned a sporting goods store in Manhattan and with whom she had starred in a film that was never completed. She had married him, she told me, to get away from her manic depressive mother.

My father recalled that after "one thing led to another," in March 1935, he and my mother "escaped to the British Virgin Is-

My mother, photographed by my father in the British Virgin Islands, 1935

My mother, British Virgin Islands, 1935

lands" (Tortola and Guana) for over a month. "We came up here [to the Rollins cabin on Horseleech Pond] after we got back from the islands and she had gone to Reno for a divorce." My father always chuckled when he remembered that he had three women getting divorced in Reno at the same time. Beside my mother, there was his wife Helen Schroeder, and the married woman with whom he had had the affair. My parents married in 1936.

Back on Horseleech Pond, my father and mother began to expand Rollins's cabin. My father believed that houses should not interfere with nature. Our house was painted gray so that it would be almost invisible to someone walking in the woods. Room after room stretched across the brow of a small hill overlooking the pond. We called it the Big House. They lived simply on a small allowance from my grandparents and occasional gifts from my father's mother, but they did manage to have milk and groceries delivered every day. With vegetables from the garden and the occasional duck shot by my father, they were, he said, "living high." In 1937 my father's mother paid for the construction of a new "babies' room," and that May, Blair was born.

To avoid Cape Cod's bleak windy winters, each year in late autumn, my father and mother piled their Cape Cod furniture into an enormous box-shaped dark green metal truck (a 1928 Dodge) they called the Blunderbus and drove to Manhattan. Because of the Depression, they could rent an unfurnished East Side brownstone or a Fifth Avenue apartment for almost no money. Once a week they gave dancing parties. My uncle Horton O'Neil remembered a party they gave in February 1940: They had decorated the living room to make the house "look like their own with easels and pieces of driftwood placed 'casually' about." They provided the music and guests brought bottles. Blair has a vague memory of a piggy bank on top of the piano into which non-bottle-toting guests could put money.

My father was supposed to be a painter. After Blair was born, he built a large studio in the shape of a lean-to on top of a sand dune overlooking the ocean. The tallest side of the studio was mostly glass. It was difficult, my father said, to paint in a place with such a beautiful view. And the wind was enervating. Years later my mother shuddered at the memory: "Oh! That wind!" she groaned. Another reason it was hard for my father to paint was that he became curious when he saw friends enjoying themselves on the beach below. I have no memory of him painting in his dune studio. Instead my parents held dancing parties there. Over time, windblown sand etched the glass until most of it was frosted. The world outside became blurred like memories of moments half-forgotten.

When I was in my twenties I went inside the abandoned studio. I was trespassing. Neither the studio nor our Big House belonged to us anymore. The studio's interior was spare and luminous, but so empty. As the sand dunes receded, the studio became cantilevered out over the beach. Then it fell down the dune. Thirty years later all that was left was a section of well pipe sticking out of the sand some ten feet from the bottom of the dune. Every time I saw that pipe there was a clench like a fist in my chest. The past is so very

My father's dune studio

past, and the present will soon be long ago. Another ten years went by and even the pipe was gone.

Perhaps because he wasn't painting, in 1939 my father took it into his head to study architecture at Harvard's Graduate School of Design. To have an example of his work to show to Walter Gropius, who headed the school, he built a flat-roofed modern house out of Homasote, a construction material that resembles thick cardboard and that is made out of recycled paper. He called it the Paper Palace. Gropius immediately pointed to the place where he could tell the house must leak. For a year my father followed the curriculum designed for second-year graduate students. But my mother persuaded him to withdraw from architectural school and to return to Horseleech Pond. It was the Depression. Not many people were building houses, she said. And in November 1940 in Boston, I was born.

My mother and father liked a lot of privacy, so their bedroom was way at one end of the Big House. Using a Japanese-style folding screen upon which she painted a series of oddly juxtaposed motifs: bi-plane, star, cloud, boat, seashell, pinwheel, Greek temple, and open book against a royal blue ground, my mother divided the bedroom in two. Half of it became her painting studio. At the other end of the house was the kitchen and a pantry/bar whose counter held glasses in various shapes and sizes and all kinds of implements that I guessed were for making drinks. I could just reach up and touch these mysterious objects. In the bar was an icebox that was filled once a week when the iceman came with his wagon full of ice. With his ice block tongs, he lifted a huge hunk of ice and carried it into our house. The ice had beautiful lines in it that looked like cracks, but the chunks he carried never fell apart.

A door in the pantry/bar led to Blair's and my bedroom wing. My room had red cotton curtains with tiny yellow and blue flowers. During naps, I liked to lie in bed watching the curtains move in a breeze. What was outside my window—trees and grass and, in the distance, beyond the scrub oak, golden dunes—mixed with what was inside and with the flowers on my curtains. When the sun turned the curtains bright red, I felt safe. No one, not even a wolf, could get past my red curtains. During the day, the dark things hanging on hooks inside my closet door lost their menace. At night, I closed my closet door so no bad person could come out.

Besides grass and trees outside my bedroom window, if I looked to the right and way down to the bottom of the hill, I could see my father's vegetable garden in a swampy area that ended where the dune rose up. My father made ditches so that the raised part of the garden was planted, and the low part turned into little canals. When he took me down to his garden to show me how to pick beets, I had to jump over the canals without landing on any beets. My father took his garden seriously. I had to be very careful. He looked so tall, so capable, and, as my mother said, so dark and handsome. I was proud of him and I was sure he could protect me if something happened.

After the dining room came the living room. It had a large corner window facing the pond. Beneath this window was a built-in seat where my mother liked to read in the afternoon. On the mantel over the fireplace was an elephant's tusk carved to look like an alligator with scales. Blair and I liked to run our fingers along the bumps and indentations on the ivory. The smooth parts were cool and made you think of all the years that had gone by since it was made by someone in China. Our father told us not to drop it. It was precious. Usually he didn't care about material things, but this tusk he loved. When we played the game of jumping off the mantel onto sofa pillows spread over the floor, we had to remove the tusk first.

Blair's and my favorite game was to tip over chairs and take down all the cushions to build a house just big enough for us. I could crawl backward into my room and crouch in its doorway like a bear guarding his cave. When we were done, our mother always made us put the cushions and chairs back, a melancholy job. Although the living room was mostly for grownups, we were allowed to listen to a record of Sergei Prokofiev's *Peter and the Wolf*. The music went perfectly with the voice telling the story—it sounded scary when the wolf approached and it sounded funny when the wolf swallowed a duck whole and the duck kept quacking. Peter's wolf was more dangerous than the wolves in *Little Red Riding Hood* or *The Three Little Pigs*. But I liked to be scared. As long as Blair was there beside me, I knew that the story was not real.

Our mother had a beautiful speaking voice, cool and clear with a slight English accent, which made her sound superior. But she had a terrible singing voice, so she never sang. It must have been our father who taught us songs: "Mary Had a Little Lamb," "The Bear Went over the Mountain," "On Top of Old Smokey," and "Yankee Doodle Went to Town." In my mind, these songs were stories and I could picture everything that happened. I saw Mary's snow-white lamb following her to school. I saw a brown bear reaching the top of a mountain and looking sad because the other side was just the same as the world he already knew. But there was one song that I sang over and over and that put no pictures in my head. The words sounded like nonsense: "Mairzy doats and dozy doats and liddle lamzy divey, A kiddley divey too, wooden shoe?" Years would pass before I could decipher the meaning of these syllables. It turned out to be all about what mares, does, lambs, and kids eat. I liked the song better when I didn't know what it meant.

2

Friends

My parents invited their upper bohemian friends for cocktails or dinner. Most of these were people born to privilege but chose an unconventional way of life. My father recalled: "The back woods were very, very neighborly in the Forties, and there were about fifty people in the three towns of Wellfleet, Truro, and Provincetown that one saw." I loved it when guests came. All afternoon my mother would be in a good mood, washing lettuce and preparing something like a thick pea soup with cut-up carrots and linguiça floating in it. She always made hot buttered garlic bread with a long loaf that came from the Portuguese bakery in Provincetown. During the cocktail hour Blair carried around a bowl of peanuts. I followed her around carrying nothing. The grownups chirped like a flock of birds. I never knew what they were saying, and I didn't care.

My parents' best friends, Anna and Norman Matson, lived on the same dirt road as we did. Norman was a writer. Years later my mother told me that Hemingway had modeled the hero of *A Farewell to Arms* on Norman, so he must have been more interesting than he seemed to me. He was much older than Anna, and less loving. Maybe he was too old to care about children. Once when I spent the night at the Matsons' house, Anna put me in a room next to Norman's. In the middle of the night I heard something that sounded like a growling wolf. Rigid with terror, I pulled the blankets over my head and did not move. In the morning Anna told me that the sound was just Norman snoring. When my father painted Anna's portrait, it was agreed that Norman would pay for it if a play he had written and that was being produced in New York was a hit. If the play flopped, my father would pay Anna forty cents an hour for posing. At some point during these years, Anna and my father are said to have had an affair, one which neither of them took very seriously.

Anna was my mother's best friend. She was at the Big House all the time, and she was like an extra mother to Blair and me. Her mother, Anna Strunsky, was a Russian Jewish immigrant and

Anna Matson, c. 1940

The Matson family: Norman, Anna, Little Anna, a friend, and Peter, 1951

a prominent Socialist. Anna's father, William English Walling, belonged to a wealthy Louisville family but turned to Socialism, worked as a labor reformer, and helped to found the National Association for the Advancement of Colored People (NAACP). Anna must have inherited her parents' social conscience. For years, she worked for the International Refugee Committee. Perhaps it was she who placed a German refugee couple in my parents' home in 1939. The man served drinks and helped with dinners and with the vegetable garden. His wife cleaned and took care of Blair and me. I do not remember what either of them looked like, but they must have been nice to us, for I can see from photographs that we were happy.

In her social activism, Anna was the opposite of my mother, who never read the newspaper and who took no interest in current events. In our house, politics was a dirty word, almost as bad as golf. My mother disdained business and businessmen, too. All she cared about was art and music and books.

On the shore of Slough, the pond next to Horseleech, my father built a one-bedroom cottage with the help of a man named Howard Snow. When the building was almost finished, Snow looked down from the roof's peak where he was nailing the final shingles, and said to my father: "Well, Jack, it's a nice little place you have here, but it's on my land!" Fortunately, Snow was mistaken. My father called the episode "A kind of New England joke."

He rented the cottage to the Russian-born architect Serge Chermayeff and his English wife, Barbara, who, with their two sons, had immigrated to the United States in 1940. Chermayeff liked it so much that in 1944 he bought it. Serge and Barbara became lifelong friends. Barbara was mild and soft-spoken, but Serge frightened me—he was very tall, and he had a huge hook nose, a commanding voice, and piercing eyes. All he had to do was stand up and there was drama in the air. He was famous for his temper.

When my parents visited the Chermayeffs, they kept Blair and me out of the way. Perhaps because we were not allowed in the house, what I remember best about the Chermayeffs' place in the 1940s was the outhouse. Its seat was painted white and it had two holes cut into it, a big one for adults and a small one for children. This seemed to me to be so thoughtful, so kind.

The Chermayeffs' younger son, Peter (b. 1936), recently told me that his father once walked along the edge of Slough Pond to deliver ice to a voluptuous woman, a sculptor named Gitou Knoop, who was staying in a house on the same pond. When Gitou came to the door, there was Serge, holding ice tongs with a huge block of dripping ice. He was stark naked.

Like many of my parents' Cape Cod friends, the Chermayeffs thought their children could fend for themselves. In 1940, when Serge and Barbara went to San Francisco to see about a teaching job for Serge, they left their two sons with Walter Gropius. After the California job came through, Serge wrote to Gropius and asked

Serge Chermayeff with Marcel Breuer on
Chermayeff's deck, 1980

him to send the boys. Gropius had misgivings: Ivan Chermayeff was eight and Peter was four. The trip to San Francisco would take four days and require four changes of train. But Serge arranged for Catholic nuns across the country to meet and supervise the boys at the stations where they had to change trains. "And my father was an atheist!" Peter observed.

Other friends such as the highly regarded literary critic and editor, Edmund Wilson and his then wife Mary McCarthy, came from across Route 6. McCarthy put my father (conflated with another male friend) in *A Charmed Life*, her bitter 1955 novel about Wellfleet and Truro's bohemia. I don't think she had much respect for my father or for any of the artists and writers in the Wellfleet/Truro community. In a story called "The Lost Weekend" she described Wellfleet (which she called Nottingham) as "a kind of asylum for the derelicts of the American creative life . . ." Most of these "charming" people, she wrote, were trying to ignore their "failure of talent." Although my father had a quick wit and knew

Edmund Wilson and Mary McCarthy

everything about nature, he was not a man who talked about literature, politics, or ideas. He was a talented flirt whose seductive manner delighted all the beautiful women. Maybe witnessing my father's charm at work on others irritated McCarthy, who always liked to be the center of attention.

Edmund Wilson was what my mother, in a disparaging tone of voice, called "a big intellectual." He had served as editor for *Vanity Fair* and *The New Republic*. His literary criticism appeared in *The New Yorker* magazine as well as in his brilliant book *Axel's Castle* (1931). He took a keen interest in politics, and in *To Finland Station* (1940) he examined the development of socialism from 1824 to 1917. No doubt he thought of my parents as intellectual lightweights. In a diary entry for June 18, 1940, Wilson wrote: "It seemed to me that people like Margaret Bishop [writer John Peale Bishop's wife] and Jack Phillips and his wife, who probably thought they were anti-Fascists, were becoming more aggressive in response to the Nazi successes."

Wilson was also a man who enjoyed extramarital affairs. (His friend Leon Edel, who edited some of Wilson's diaries, called him a "roving bohemian.") Perhaps his friendship with my parents had something to do with my mother's beauty. My father's memories of Wilson and McCarthy were gently scornful. One of his favorite stories was about the night Wilson and McCarthy came for supper and, when they drove home, a roll of chicken wire fencing got caught on the back bumper of their old Chevy. As they progressed along the dirt road that leads from Horseleech Pond to Route 6, the wire unrolled behind them. My father delighted in visualizing the discomfited (and probably inebriated) Wilson having to cope with detaching the wire from his car in the dark. Another time, my parents were driving past a swimming beach on Slough Pond when they spotted McCarthy and Wilson about to set a match to a pile of kindling upon which they planned to cook a picnic lunch.

My father was horrified. There had been a long drought and the day was windy. The forest could have gone up in flames as it had in 1922 when many acres in Wellfleet and Truro burned. My father jumped out of his car and told them not to light the fire. Wilson was angry. "Why not come over to our house for the cookout?" my father suggested, but "They sort of went off in a huff."

Another misadventure with Wilson and McCarthy happened in the late 1930s when my father and mother picked mushrooms for a mushroom feast to which they invited ten or twelve friends. "Edmund and Mary, probably the Jencks . . ." were among the guests, my father recalled. The musician Gardner Jencks and his wife, Ruth (nastily portrayed in McCarthy's *The Charmed Life*), lived in a house overlooking the bay way out on Bound Brook Island. Most likely Charles and Adelaide Walker came, too. Charles Walker was a writer, historian, and editor who, in 1922 had written *Steel: The Diary of a Furnace Worker* about his own youthful labors in a steel mill in 1919. In 1933, with his wife, Adelaide, he founded the Theater Union, a downtown Manhattan performing group. "We had something with mushrooms in it," my father remembered, "a soup or a stew. . . . Well, I must have picked *russula emetica*, with its pink-ribbed cap: it would only take about one of them to make people sick. They sort of left the table and went home: our dinner was soon over. Only Lybie and I weren't sick—it sort of puzzled us. It was considered, of course, a disaster."

In June 1942, my father rented the Paper Palace to the Surrealists Matta Echaurren, Max Ernst, and Ernst's wife, gallerist Peggy Guggenheim. These tenants taught my parents Surrealist games, the erotic nature of which shocked my father. He recalled that in the game of Truth and Consequences, if you chose consequences, you might be required to masturbate in front of the assembled players. My father was not enthusiastic. He didn't care that the Surrealists thought he was a stuffed shirt. "They were very theatri-

Paper Palace designed by my father in 1939 and occupied by
Max Ernst, Matta Echaurren, and Peggy Guggenheim in 1942

cal. They made me nervous, but they weren't boring. . . . I think my
wife joined in some of the games they were always playing. Peggy
Vail [Peggy Guggenheim's daughter] was doing transformations of
bottles and I remember Max Ernst swinging a can of paint with
holes punched in the bottom over a canvas spread on the kitchen
floor. . . . Matta used to go about with a little walking stick and a
kerchief. I thought he was absolutely riveting, full of energy and
very friendly. Matta did a lot of painting up there, and [Abstract
Expressionist painter, Robert] Motherwell, who arrived looking
very gray flannel suit, seemed very impressed by his work."

Both Ernst and Matta got into trouble with the FBI. Ernst was
a German émigré, thus suspect. One day he went into the woods
to burn trash, and the police came around. "You have been sending
up smoke signals to the enemy," they said. "Did you know that just
a few days ago an American ship was sunk nearby by a Nazi submarine?" The FBI questioned Ernst about whether Matta had been
using the Paper Palace's shutters to send signals to German sub-

marines. They also suspected that Matta had been climbing onto the Paper Palace's flat roof in order to communicate with submarines. An agent asked Ernst how many ladders Matta had. Hearing "letters" instead of "ladders," Ernst said, "Five: M-A-T-T-A." In the end, Ernst had to go to Boston for further questioning. Peggy Guggenheim accompanied him and brought an end to the ordeal by telling the authorities that she was a copper heiress. All it took was a phone call and Ernst was free to go.

My father came under suspicion, too. During the war he was driving to the Big House after picking up my mother from the train station and he noticed a car following him. The car came all the way into the woods and out of it came agents of the FBI. The officers assumed the Navajo blanket that my father had thrown in the back of his car in case my mother felt cold must be hiding guns. Its design resembled a swastika. When my father explained that this was a Native American motif, all was well. Another time, the Wellfleet police chief, who did occasional handyman's work, was installing lanterns in the Big House and he noticed that my father had a gun rack. "A few days later," my father recalled, "the house was surrounded by a small army, led by a lieutenant who came to look for 'Nazi guns.' Well, they discovered they were antiques."

3

Turkey Farm

The chicken wire fence that attached itself to Edmund Wilson's car was farm equipment. My father raised turkeys during the war. He had experimented with turkeys before the war, raising one hundred chicks in his dune studio. With the help of Anna Matson's younger brother, a conscientious objector named Hayden Walling, my father constructed ten turkey brooder houses out of two-by-fours and Homasote board and he placed them on the hillside overlooking the ocean, a four-minute uphill walk from our house. "We got about 3,000 chicks through the mail," my father told an interviewer. "Given the usual mortalities from disease or predators, we ended up with 2,600 brown birds. . . . After the chicks had grown up, we put them out behind the fencing wire. . . . All this kept Hayden [Walling] and me busy."

When he first took me up the hill and showed me his turkeys, the brooder house floors were covered with fuzzy yellow chicks whose voices merged into one beseeching wail. It was alarming. I wanted to pick up one but didn't. My mother later told me that my father had raised turkeys to avoid going to war. Being married and the thirty-four-year–old father of two children, he did not want to enlist.

He had participated in the war already. When the United States entered World War II in December 1941 our family was spending the winter in New York City and my father went to work designing camouflage at the Brooklyn Navy Yard. The job seemed pointless: radar was making camouflage obsolete and the design aspect of camouflage work was drying up. In any case, he hated working in an office. He was an outdoors man, and prolonged periods in confined interiors made him desperate. When he got home at night he was depressed and angry, which was not good for his marriage. Years later, my father remembered that: "My immediate boss, a Navy commander, wanted to get me into a two-striped lieutenant's uniform and I realized it was an awfully stupid job. . . . So I quit and came up here and had a turkey farm going in no time flat, as part of the war effort." Becoming a farmer and selling turkeys to the troops gave him an exemption. His mother criticized his choice and praised her younger son, Arthur, who served as a fighter pilot and who escaped death by disobeying the orders of the officer in charge of an aircraft carrier who sent his pilots up in spite of terrible weather. When they tried to land on the carrier, several planes fell into the sea. When it was his turn, my uncle decided to fly his plane to shore. The commander was "kicked upstairs" and my uncle's military career soon ended.

In the midst of the brooder houses was a very different kind of house, eight-foot square with weathered wooden walls and glassless windows. As a child, I never knew what this house was for. Because it had no purpose, I thought of it as mine, my safe place, my fort. Later I learned that Dr. Rollins had built it as a lookout. His journal entry for November 14, 1927, tells us that on the bluff overlooking the ocean, he found old bricks and other vestiges of a ruined building, which he surmised must be from a halfway house erected as a refuge for shipwrecked sailors. With his friend Leslie Newcomb, he built "a rough structure with windows on three sides and a glass in the door on the west, so I can sit there and see the surf. I am so old I get chilled there in too short a time; for high surf means high wind, and when comparatively calm at camp, it may be fifty miles an hour there. It is the best view I have . . . I can get there in a few minutes." I could get there from the Big House in a few minutes, too, but the windswept hilltop felt thousands of miles away from home. It felt brave to be up there on the treeless hill covered with bearberry, poverty grass, and a few strands of beach grass. Through the window that faced the ocean I could watch for German submarines.

For my father, this small house was a place to get out of the rain or to keep an eye out for predators. Indeed, there were predators, foxes, of course, and weasels and raccoons, but the worst were the great horned owls. They bit the heads off our turkeys. My father hired nine-year-olds Ivan Chermayeff and Charles Walker (the son of Charles and Adelaide) to spend nights at the turkey farm and keep watch. Ivan recalled being equipped with a gun with which to shoot owls. The owls prevailed. Peter Chermayeff remembers the horror of coming up the hill and seeing headless turkeys with bloody necks lying all over the ground.

While my father dealt with his turkeys, I stood in the look-out house listening to the ocean and watching clouds move in and out of my view. Sometimes I imagined that I lived here all alone. I moved my eyes over the hill and wondered what I could find to eat. Bearberry, an evergreen ground cover that looks like cranberry, has little red berries that taste awful. I could find blueberries, yes; they grew at the bottom of the hill, closer to the pond, and maybe a fish. This kind of thought made me glad when my father finished his turkey chores and took me home for supper.

About a mile to the north of the turkey farm, just where a deer path leading from the west end of Horseleech Pond to the ocean beach comes out at the top of a dune, there used to be another small house that Blair and I played in. This one was said to have once been a sailors' halfway house. During the war, it was used by the Coast Guard to watch for German submarines. The Coast Guard drove Jeeps along a sand road that ran on the tops of the dunes all the way from Newcomb's Hollow Beach to Ballston Beach. Now, after years of wind and waves blasting the dunes, the Coast Guard road has fallen into the sea.

I used to dream that a German submarine rose out of the water and came toward our beach. As Germans clambered out of their boat, I ran up the dune, which, in my dream was immense and had an overhang that made it impossible to reach the top. Sand kept sliding so that no matter how hard I tried, I made no progress. And now the Germans were climbing the dune behind me. I needed to scale the dune and run down to the safety of our pond, but I couldn't move. That was the point when I always woke up.

My father impressed me as a man who could do anything. He could build houses. He could go deer hunting accompanied by our beloved red setter, Hamlet. In winter, he could sail across the frozen pond by attaching a sail to his khaki-green duck boat. One year he bought a huge army Jeep and he drove Blair and me across land that had no roads on Great Island, a pine-covered peninsula that juts out into Wellfleet's bay. In the autumn, he would kill turkeys and hang them by their legs on a wooden frame just below our front steps. When they were ready, he knew how to pluck them, too. And our father had a daring stunt that he performed at dull moments during parties and that, if we begged, he would do for Blair and me. All six-foot-two of him would be standing straight with his arms pinned to his sides and he would suddenly fall forward, stiff as a board. He would then get up and smile at our alarm. Later I learned that a second before hitting the floor he put his hands forward to break his fall.

He was good at making dwellings. Once while the Blunderbus was parked just below the front steps of the Big House, my father turned its back cabin into a room complete with a woodstove, a rug, and two cots. For a week or so—maybe when our parents had guests who needed our rooms—Blair and I got to live in the Blunderbus. It was like playing house. We felt so grown up, so independent. One winter the snow came higher than the Big House windows. Our father shoveled a narrow path that wound its way downhill from our kitchen door. When I walked on it, all I could see was the tops of trees and the sky. Just to the left of the Big House's front steps he made an igloo by tunneling into a drift. Blair and I crawled inside and were surprised to find how cozy it was. It wouldn't be that bad to be an Eskimo.

This must have been the snowstorm of December 1942, probably the same storm that, years later, my father told me about, a storm that felled trees and made it impossible to drive out of the woods. The Matsons, he recalled, were running out of food and their pipes froze so they moved in with us and shared our meals of turkey—the headless turkeys left by the owls needed to be consumed. When the storm cleared, there was a note in the local newspaper saying that the Phillips family was "down to their last turkey." A letter from my mother to her mother-in-law written just after what was probably the same storm said that my father, because he had to go to work at the Brooklyn Navy Yard, had walked out to the bus pulling his belongings on a toboggan. Our heating oil ran out and we all lived in the kitchen and living room which were heated with wood. Finally, the Coast Guard came and helped by carrying me, some toys, and our luggage to Newcomb's Hollow Beach where a taxi transported my mother and Blair and me to a train. My mother was amused when all the newspapers on the East Coast carried the story: "Nine people cut off in woods on Ocean Beach. Food dwindling, oil gone."

After escaping the snowy woods, we went to New York and moved into an unfurnished apartment. Once the town had ploughed our dirt road, the Blunderbus brought our furniture. Since my grandmother was always complaining that my parents lived too expensively, my mother explained to her in a letter that the reason they rented an unfurnished apartment was because furnished ones cost over $200 a month. "Try to make a budget of $360 a month and include schools, maid, food, liquor, doctors, children's clothes, entertainment, Jack's lunches, electricity, gas, telephone, drugs etc. and see how much is left for rent."

Instead of painting in his dune studio, my father liked to build alternative places to live in and to serve as rental properties. He decided to hire a bulldozer to clear a road to the other end of Horseleech Pond where he planned to build a camp. He was getting tired of turkeys. "By our third or fourth year," he recalled, "problems arose—and I had to market the surviving turkeys before they were fully grown." Making dwellings seemed like a better idea. When the rough dirt road was finished, you could walk from our Big House to the west end of Horseleech Pond. If you looked to the right, through oak trees, you could see sunlit dunes. If you looked left, there were glimpses of our pond.

When I was maybe five or six, I had a dream about being in the back of my father's open army Jeep with my mother at the wheel and Blair beside her. They talked in the most casual way as the Jeep plowed through the forest where the not-yet-built road would be.

My mother in the window seat in the
Big House living room, c. 1942

I was shocked by my mother's lack of concern as she drove straight up each tree trunk and down the other side. She never bothered to go around. By some magic stronger than gravity the Jeep did not fall. Nothing scared my mother. She wanted her daughters to be undaunted, but her blithe attitude frightened me.

My father was not always brave. He was afraid of heights. He told me that once he had climbed down a mountain to a ledge where he discovered that he couldn't go further down, nor could he climb back up. I don't know how he finally escaped, but his story left me with a terror of narrow ledges and precipices. Also, I think he was afraid of rats. Off the short hallway that led to Blair's and my bedrooms was a door that opened onto cellar stairs. I had never been down there. It was a dark and scary place. One evening, when he heard scurrying noises coming from the cellar, our father flew into a rage against varmints and went down with his gun and shot rats.

Other animals that irritated my father were my mother's baby pigs. She maintained that pigs were intelligent and adorable. Without consulting my father, she accepted two piglets from a friend, and she made a pen for them. Some of the time she let them loose in the house. She was not squeamish and didn't mind picking up their droppings. But my father was furious when they rooted about in his vegetable garden. Years later he told me that when my mother went to New York City, probably to see a lover, he became so fed up with her pigs that he put them in her closet. They had diarrhea. When my mother returned, opened her closet, and saw her ruined clothes, she said nothing. No reproach at all. I guess she felt guilty about her trip.

Things had not been going well between my parents since the miserable period when he was working at the Brooklyn Navy Yard. It was probably then that my mother began a love affair with a scientist named George Senseney whom she met through my father's younger sister, Madelyn O'Neil. My uncle Horton O'Neil recalled that in the spring of 1943, he and Madelyn had cocktails with my parents at Manhattan's New Weston Bar. They were joined by George Senseney, an old friend of Horton's. After about three drinks each, everyone was, Horton said, "fairly crocked. . . . George and Lybie got into a cab to leave and Jack, in trying to go with them very nearly pulled the door off its hinges."

By the summer of 1943 my parents were separated. From Cornwall, Connecticut, my mother wrote to my father's mother saying that she was sorry that the marriage had failed. Blair and I were, she said, "well and good and happy . . . easier to manage, calmer and sweeter than ever before." She attributed this improvement to her own contentment. But, she said, "Hayden has boils. . . . She is incredibly good and patient about them even when they are most painful." She told her mother-in-law that Blair and I would go to Dalton in the fall. "Hayden yearns for school. She looks just like Jack and is adorable."

My grandmother wrote back (August 30, 1943): "I think that you both have made a fetish of your own happiness and that seems ironically to defeat its own ends. You had a lot to put up with, for you were not meant for domesticity and solitude and should marry a rich man." On that same date, my father wrote his mother that he and our mother were "trying to adjust the children as gradually as possible." Sometimes we stayed in the Big House with both our parents, and sometimes our father came to see us after our mother took us to live in New York in October 1943. That fall he stayed on Horseleech Pond. When it got too cold, he moved to Manhattan. My parents applied for a divorce in the Barnstable Court. In those days, cruel and abusive treatment was grounds for divorce. "He put pigs in my closet," my mother told the judge. The divorce was granted on July 11, 1944.

4

Divorce

For a long time after my mother left him, my father was sad. He thought that if he just waited, she and George Senseney would tire of each other. He arranged a meeting with George's red-haired wife and tried to persuade her to keep calm and wait. But she was in such a fury that divorce was the only answer. My father thought his marriage was a good one. My mother's intelligence, beauty, and strength made life interesting. He enjoyed her adventurous approach to the body. She was fearless, game for anything. Years later he still maintained that she was the right wife for him. They came from similar backgrounds. They both wanted to live simply, to be close to nature, and to paint. In addition, they had two small daughters. The marriage should have worked.

Even if he had waited, my mother probably would not have gone back to him. Sexual desire was not the problem. It was my father's lack of drive. It made him seem weak. He had just enough money from a family allowance to not have to work for a living, and he didn't work hard at being an artist. My mother liked men with ambition, men like George Senseney who bristled with energy.

My father was not a man to stay long without female companionship. In February 1944 he met Dasya Chaliapin, the twenty-three-year-old divorced daughter of the renowned Russian opera singer Feodor Chaliapin. In January 9, 1945, from his apartment at 1407 Third Avenue, he wrote to his mother that he was about to

marry Dasya, whom he described as "a lovely, talented creature—
of great warmth."

Occasionally our father would collect Blair and me and take us
to Central Park. I do not remember ever visiting him in the apartment he shared with Dasya. During our first autumn in New York,
he photographed us in the park with Hamlet. We were so happy
to see our Cape Cod dog again and happy to see our father, too.
He was attentive. We did our best to be jolly because he was sad.
We tried to be good children so that he would stay with us forever.

Me in Central Park, NY, with Hamlet, 1944

Blair, Hamlet, and me, Central Park, 1944

In the mid-1940s, my father made a series of black-and-white etchings that reflected his unhappy state of mind and his distaste for city life. He set up a small printing press in Dasya's mother's apartment on Central Park South. The etchings he produced were as sardonic and bitter as George Grosz's caricatural images of decadence in 1920s Berlin. Some prints had a similar cast of characters: prostitutes, fat lascivious businessmen, alcoholics at a cabaret. One etching was of a subway car packed with naked people holding on to leather straps. My favorite was of an apartment building imagined as if one whole wall were removed. In the grid of small square rooms, he drew naked men and women—some of them up to no good. In 1947, one of his etchings graced the cover of *Life* magazine and, thanks to Serge Chermayeff, who was now president of Chicago's Institute of Design, the Art Institute of Chicago gave my father an exhibition.

To make these prints he invented a new etching technique. My father had a scientific bent—something encouraged, no doubt, by his father and by Dr. Rollins—and printmaking allowed him to experiment with different chemicals and different ways of drawing on the copper plate. He mostly avoided color. He was, I think, afraid of self-expression. Carrying on about your own emotions seemed self-absorbed and vulgar to him. Most of his subsequent art explored the landscape. He was steeped in Thoreau. He wanted his images to be about the observation of nature—not nature filtered through a temperament, but nature itself.

When he was in the Big House, my father had various projects to keep him busy. He moved six small turkey brooder houses and set them along the shore at the west end of Horseleech Pond, the place where the road he had bulldozed between the ocean and the pond ended. Five turkey houses became bedrooms. The sixth, placed behind the others, served as a bathroom. He named the pine needle path in front of the five bedroom houses Commercial Street

Turkey Houses

and the path in front of the bathroom Bradford Street. These were
the names of the two main streets in Provincetown. For a living
room/kitchen he built a one-room, eighteen-by-twenty-foot cinder block house with a roof that pitched upward toward the pond.
The wall that looked out onto the pond was mostly glass. In the
middle was a fireplace. My father explained that the house resembled a lean-to and the fireplace was like the fire in front of a
lean-to's opening that a camper might light in order to keep out
wild animals at night. On the pond side of the building he added
a perfectly proportioned porch whose front edge, depending on
rainfall, was only two or three feet from the shore.

We began to spend summers at this camp, which we called the
Turkey Houses. At first, I missed the Big House. It was a real house
with real walls, and with one room leading to another. The turkey
houses were shacks, just barely shelters. Instead of a hallway we had
pine-needle-covered paths. We had to go outside to go to the bathroom and at night, I tried not to run from the bathroom back to my
cabin, because if I did run, I saw murderers behind every bush. A
few years later, my father's fourth wife persuaded my father to sell
the Big House. This was a loss. Even now, when I swim or canoe

across the pond, I get a momentary pang when I look up through the trees to see the patches of gray clapboarding that, eighty years ago, my father nailed up. The Big House is the place where my mother and father were together. And they seemed happy.

After the war my father bought a group of prefabricated, portable army barracks. They were military surplus, thus cheap. The only big expense was shipping them from Georgia, which cost $400. Although he was averse to spending money, these could be rental houses and he could live on the income. The summer before the houses were shipped, my father took me to the places where he might put them. Three would be built on Slough Pond (about three hundred feet from Horseleech), and two were to go on the dunes overlooking the ocean.

Walking along Slough Pond's shore with our feet in the water, my father and I stopped at possible house sites. When he asked me if I thought this or that patch of land would be a good place for a home, I always said yes, even though the only kind of house that I could picture so near the pond was a stick hut, like Eeyore's in *Winnie the Pooh*. I stepped carefully, trying not to crush the pickerel reeds with their pointed purple flowers and making sure not to splash and scare away any turtle that might be sunning himself on a broken branch. Bullfrogs leapt into the water as we passed. My father didn't like frogs. They kept him awake at night, so one summer he caught some big ones and put them into Slough Pond. Maybe these frogs that were now jumping away from our footfalls were those exiled frogs, but the racket that Horseleech Pond frogs still made at night made me wonder if the bullfrogs had returned home.

When in the middle of winter, the army barracks arrived at the Wellfleet depot on a flatbed open rail car, their disassembled parts were warped and stuck together from exposure to rain in the South and then freezing temperatures in the North. It took a backhoe to pry the frozen sections apart and to lift them off the train. My father bulldozed roads to the houses' sites and, one home at a time, the barracks were placed on a trailer and towed by a tractor into the woods. After putting the sections together, he added fireplaces, bathrooms, and concrete patios. For several years my father rented these cottages and then he sold them, most often to his tenants. The house on the hill was sold to an architect named Henry Hebbeln. The next house went to editor and film critic, Dwight Macdonald and his wife, Nancy, and the third one was bought by Peter and Vita Petersen (he was involved with export, and she was a painter) who six years later sold a half share to Arthur Schlesinger Jr. and his wife, Marian. What we lost in privacy was made up for by having lively company. The children who lived in these houses became lifelong friends.

Dwight Macdonald, c. 1950

5

Manhattan

When our mother picked Blair and me up from the Big House and took us to live in New York City in 1943 we did not at first live with her. She parked in front of a six-story building on Ninety-Sixth Street just east of Third Avenue and we climbed dark and windowless stairs to the apartment she had rented on the fifth floor. Our mother rang the buzzer, and Ellie opened the door. Ellie was an Irish woman she had hired to look after us. She had curly white hair held in place by a hairnet. Her pale, wrinkled skin sagged into folds at the bottom of her face, and it jiggled on the inside of her upper arms. Her hands moved a lot when she talked to our mother. To us she didn't say much more than hello. Our mother had told us how much fun we were going to have with Ellie. Ellie didn't look mean, but I wasn't sure. Some old ladies in fairy tales want to put children in the oven or make them go to sleep for a hundred years.

When our mother finished talking to Ellie, she bent down, kissed us each on the cheek, turned, and stood with her back to us in the doorway. Her body filled the opening. To me she was golden, luminous like the sun, different from our father who was silver like our pond. Her shoulders were set. She did not look back. I wanted to hold onto her, but I knew she wouldn't like it, so I just stood watching the top of her head disappear down the stairs. This is when I learned to squeeze my heart into a stone. Nothing can touch me. I am somewhere else. What is happening is not happening to me. When I lost sight of my mother, I tried to be like her and to tell myself that everything would be wonderful. I thought of food: yes, Ellie would cook us a delicious supper with ice cream for dessert.

Ellie liked me, but she did not like Blair. I could tell because she let me sit on her lap and not Blair. When she brushed my hair, she would pat my head, and if I had a tangle, she would carefully work the hairs loose with her fingers so that it didn't hurt. I was about to turn three, and I had a round face, blond hair, hazel eyes, and a wide smile that showed the gaps between my front teeth. Everything new in life enthralled me. Blair had long brown hair, blue eyes, and perfect classical features, but she was not jolly like me. Ellie used to trim our nails and save the little quarter moons that she cut off. "I'm keeping these," she explained, "because when your mother comes, I can show them to her, and she will know that I am taking good care of you."

Me and Blair, New York, 1943

When our mother came to see us, she brought chocolate éclairs from a nearby bakery. Or she brought presents, for me one of those push toys with a short pole attached to a cylindrical wooden cage containing small red, yellow, and blue balls. Pushing my toy down the hall and making the bouncing balls go *pop, pop, pop,* I felt so proud of myself, so strong. Every time our mother visited, she had to leave before reading a second story. If I begged her to stay, she got that angry look. I stopped asking.

After a while our mother came and packed our suitcases. From now on we were going to live with her, she said. My chest pumped up with gratitude. She really wanted us. I was not at all sad to say good-bye to Ellie. My mother was the best person in the world. I loved the way she walked. I loved the way she talked. Her voice was a song. We took a taxi to 124 East Eighty-Fifth Street where she had been living. In the taxi, she explained that she had a new husband. His name was George Senseney and he was a scientist. We had to climb four flights of stairs to get to our top-floor apartment. My mother called it a railroad apartment because the rooms were laid out like train cars. The living room looked north onto Eighty-Fifth Street and east toward Lexington Avenue. My mother put potted geraniums in the sunny east window. There wasn't much furniture, just a dining room table, a sofa, some ill-assorted chairs, and a Persian carpet upon which I lay and tried to count how many different kinds of flowers were woven into it. There was also a phonograph. In the late afternoon my mother played Bach and Vivaldi and sometimes Mozart. The music made all the air in the room seem peaceful, right up to the corners of the ceiling.

The adjoining room, open to the living room, was meant to be a dining room, but my mother and George had put a big bed in there. Over the bed hung a red and orange paper butterfly kite from Chinatown. Blair and I bounced on our mother's bed but after a few months, after our mother and George started bickering,

Me, c. 1946

both the bed and the butterfly began to have a bad atmosphere, so we stopped.

After this bedroom came a long narrow hall off which were doors to the rest of the rooms. The first room was full of George's electronic machines. They were huge and scary. We were not allowed to go into that room alone. He showed us how one of the machines worked. He called it an oscillograph. If you made a sound, wiggly lines of green light came on the screen, and if you made different noises the green lines changed shape. George was a specialist in radar. Sometimes he vanished without telling us where he was going. He went out west on secret missions. Later my mother told me he had worked for the Manhattan Project and he was at Los Alamos when they exploded a bomb in July 1945.

After George's equipment room came my bedroom. It had a window looking out onto the building next door plus a small high up window that opened onto our long hall. Then, at the south end of the hall were the bathroom, the kitchen, and Blair's room. Blair's room was almost as big as the living room and it had an upright piano against the far wall. Blair took piano lessons. When I was old enough, I did, too, but I didn't get much further than Diller-Quaile exercises and "Twinkle, Twinkle, Little Star." Sometimes Blair had to move out of her room when our mother took a paying guest. The only paying guest I remember was a handsome young Swiss man named Hans von Somethingorother, who had sailed alone across the ocean in a small boat. Blair had a crush on him. I was in awe of him, so I didn't dare open my mouth in his presence.

My mother must have been doing her friend Nemone Balfour Gurievitch a favor—this man was Nemone's lover. I do not know whether Nemone knew that around 1943 my mother had an affair with her husband David Gurievitch, the Russian-born doctor who became such an intimate friend of Eleanor Roosevelt. If Nemone knew, I guess it didn't matter, for she and my mother remained life-long friends. Both were rebels. Nemone astonished her aristocratic English family by becoming a singer and by marrying a Jew. She

George Senseney, c. 1945

My mother on the beach, c. 1945

sang and recorded Scottish, English, and Irish ballads which she accompanied by playing the lute or the Irish harp. Her daughter, Grania Gurievitch, was and is my oldest friend. At Nemone's musicals, Grania and I tried to look attentive, but the songs' romantic intensity and Nemone's earnest face were embarrassing.

Our apartment's kitchen was where Blair and I ate breakfast and sometimes supper. On the left was a dumbwaiter. If you opened its door there were ropes on a pulley so that you could pull a box-like thing into which you had placed your groceries from the first to the fifth floor. Blair and I were scared of the darkness inside the dumbwaiter. What if a burglar got in and hoisted himself up to our apartment? Outside the kitchen's southern window was a fire escape and to the right of it were ropes with laundry pinned to them. These loops of rope stretched from the side of our building to the side of the next building. The neighborhood was all connected by laundry lines. Once our mother tried hanging laundry on our line, but she soon gave up. In those days, there was so much soot in the city that clean clothes had to be shaken out before putting them away.

We lived in this apartment from 1943 to 1948. Blair and I started going to the Dalton School on Eighty-Ninth Street between Park and Lexington Avenues. When we walked to school Blair was supposed to make sure I waited for the streetlights to turn green, but, being three and a half years older than me, she walked much faster and from half a block away she ignored my wails. "Wait for me!" I cried, using two notes, a high note for "wait for" and then a lower drawn out note for "meeee."

Dalton in those days emphasized the arts. There was painting class in which we wore blue smocks and stood at child-size easels brushing poster paint onto big sheets of inexpensive paper. For music, we sat on the floor in a circle playing tambourines, drums, and triangles. For dance, the teacher gave us silk scarves in different colors and asked us to improvise movements in response to music. In shop, I made a boat by nailing a little piece of wood onto a bigger piece. Blair made something much better, a box that she painted sky blue with pink flowers on the top. She gave it to our mother.

When it was time for recess, we went to the school's roof where there were green wooden boxes big enough for two or three children to climb inside. If you put a few boxes together you could build a house. I spent most of my time in a box because the boys always zoomed around in little cars and I was afraid they would crash into me. When my mother received a report on how I was doing at Dalton, it said I was not aggressive enough because I hid in boxes. At nap time we lay on blankets and the teacher turned off the lights and pulled down the shades. I liked this time of not having to say or do anything. I practiced braiding on my plaid blanket's fringe. My mother had just taught me braiding, also how to tie my shoes. The second step of shoe tying—making a loop with one shoelace, going around it with the other, and then making the final loop—was hard. When I finally succeeded, I felt almost grown up. My mother liked it when I learned to do things for myself.

Learning to read, sounding out letters and then suddenly knowing what they spelled was the biggest thrill. The pictures in our first-grade reading books gave me a vision of a carefree world. I imagined I was Jane chasing her dog Spot across a green lawn and my mother would be standing in the doorway calling me and my brother Dick in for supper. It would be so nice, I thought, to live in a clapboard house on a tree-lined street where children could play.

6

Mountain Climber

L ife on Eighty-Fifth Street was exciting. My mother loved Central Park, especially the zoo where, after watching the seals being fed, we had lunch on the terrace of the zoo cafeteria. For dessert, our mother bought us either Cracker Jacks or animal crackers. Hard to choose. Cracker Jacks had a prize in the bottom of the box, but animal crackers had a little white string across the top of the box so you could carry it as if it were a pocketbook. At the northeast zoo exit, there was a man selling helium balloons. Having a balloon on my bedroom ceiling made me think I could live on the ceiling, too. But my balloon slowly shrank, floated downward, and ended all puckered and ugly on my floor. A short way north of the

Me rock climbing in Central Park, 1944

zoo there was a rock-covered hill that I could climb on all fours. I felt so brave, so agile. I decided that when I grew up, I would be a mountain climber.

My mother was home a lot and she taught me things—how to brush my teeth, how to wash my hair in our claw-foot bathtub. She put the shampoo on top of my head and told me to mush it around. Then she said to lie back down in the bath water to rinse it out. With my hair fanned out around my face and my ears full of water, the world vanished. I held my nose and put my head completely under water—such a private place.

Soon after moving to Eighty-Fifth Street, I had my adenoids taken out. I remember the white cloth soaked with ether being put over my nose and mouth and feeling as if I were going to suffocate. When I woke up, I was in a room alone. I was so cold I had goose bumps. My mother must have come to see me in the hospital, but I have no memory of her being at my bedside. One night I heard the echoing sounds of my mother and Blair talking as they came down the hospital hall. I was so relieved, so grateful that they had come. But before the voices reached my door, I realized that there was no mother or sister anywhere.

When I was five, I was allowed to walk to the end of our block. Once I was used to doing that, my mother said I could turn south on Park Avenue and walk as far as Eighty-Fourth Street. Finally, I was ready to go the whole way around the block without crossing any streets. Being out of sight of my mother was frightening, but the feeling of bravery made it worth it. When I made the last left turn, and there, sitting on the stoop, was my mother, I felt like a hero, but my mother did not act at all surprised. She did not know that I could spin off the world and land someplace where I knew no one, where nothing was recognizable, and I would be lost forever.

I did not fall off the world and flail around in space, but I did get lost. My mother was taking Blair and me to buy something.

Maybe Blair needed to buy shoes at the Becks shoe store on Third Avenue. Or maybe we were going to buy a miniature turtle at the Lexington Avenue pet store, but turtles always died, so maybe it was a guppy. Fish died, too. Even the salamanders that we bought at Barnum & Bailey Circus died. The only pets that survived in our apartment were Siamese cats, and our mother had three of them. I loved the vibration when they purred against my skin. It felt as if I were purring.

We started walking south on Lexington. I think my mother wanted to go over to Third, but she knew I hated the roar of the elevated trains zooming overhead. I was convinced that a train would break through the tracks and fall on top of us. Anyway, Lexington was sunnier, and there were more people going by. Blair reminded me not to step on the cracks in the sidewalk. It was a game we played: "Don't step on the cracks or you'll break your mother's back." I actually believed that my stepping on a crack could kill my mother, and if she died, I wouldn't have a home, so I was very, very careful where I stepped. This slowed me down. I stopped to look in a store window full of high-heeled shoes, not interesting to me. What was interest-

My mother and me, New York, spring 1947

ing was seeing my face reflected in the window. It was surrounded by reflections of the buildings on the other side of the street. I was in two worlds at the same time. There could be more than one world. When I closed one eye and looked at an object and then opened that eye and closed the other one, the object changed places. This was true no matter what I looked at—back and forth, back and forth, up and down. With my eyes, I could make things move.

I wanted to catch up with my mother, but she and Blair were out of sight. They had such long legs and they walked so quickly. When I reached a sign that said Eighty-Second Street I stopped. I was not supposed to cross streets alone, so I headed back toward Eighty-Third Street. No sign of my mother or Blair. I waited and waited, but they didn't come. I couldn't help it—I started to cry. It was embarrassing. People turned to look at me. I crunched my shoulders forward and hung my head so that no one could see my face.

A tall well-dressed woman came over and asked me what was the matter. I managed to tell her that I couldn't find my mother. The woman asked me if I knew where I lived. Luckily my mother had made me memorize our address. "I live at 124 East Eighty-Fifth Street," I said. The woman was calm. She acted as though it was normal for a four- or five-year-old girl to be alone on Lexington Avenue. She held my hand and we walked slowly uptown. I guess she thought that if we walked slowly enough my mother would reappear. We got all the way to 124 East Eighty-Fifth Street and still no mother or sister. I was afraid the woman would have to go off and leave me alone, but she made it seem as if she were in no hurry. She talked with the same accent as my mother, so I knew that she would take care of me. Finally, Blair and my mother came around the corner. When they reached our stoop, my mother thanked the woman, who said it was nothing. My mother barely looked at me. Blair, carrying a shopping bag, climbed the stoop and stood at the front door. The woman said good-bye, and I followed Blair and my mother up the four flights of stairs. As usual, they were faster than me. I felt angry, but also guilty. I was such a slow walker. Maybe it was my fault that I had been left behind. Still, I was sad. They didn't care. They had not even noticed that I was gone.

Most of the time I was good-tempered. If I was angry, I kept it to myself. Quite often at night, when I lay in bed not sleeping, I thought, I will kill myself, and then they will see. What they would see, I hoped, was that I was smart and talented, and not to be ignored. Or I might run away. Then they would have to look for me, and while they were looking, they would realize how much they missed me.

I liked going to bed. I was allowed to look at a picture book for a little while. If I got sleepy turning the pages, I would invent stories that took place in the hills and valleys made by my top sheet's folds. Most nights when I couldn't sleep, I rubbed the backs of my hands lightly over the bottom sheet. It felt so soft, so cozy. When I was six or seven, I started to caress my nonexistent breasts. I didn't touch my tummy much because if I did, I would feel like cutting off the roll of fat below my belly button. Sometimes I would grab the roll and squeeze and pull as if I could tear it from my body.

I daydreamed a lot, especially at night when I could fantasize without interruption. When I daydreamed, I talked inside my head. During the day, I was afraid that someone would see my lips moving and think I was crazy. Sometimes I dreamed that I was great—great at dancing, mountain climbing, painting. Once I became great, everyone—mainly my mother and sister—would admire me and be glad that they were related to me. Most of my daydreams were conversations with Benny Potter or Johnny Myers, boys in Blair's grade at Dalton on whom I had crushes. I imagined that they found me brilliant and beautiful and thin, so much so that they fell in love with me. During these daydreams, I chose my words carefully. I didn't want Benny or Johnny to be bored.

7

Scary

Our mother didn't spend much time in the kitchen. Cooking for her was improvisational. Blair and I usually ate hamburger and peas. French bread with peanut butter, mayonnaise, and slices of red onion could be lunch. When we had dinner with our mother and George, we ate in the living room with candles on the table. Often my mother cooked calf's liver or tongue. They were inexpensive and full of protein, she said. When I chewed it, I imagined that the tiny bumps on the tongue could taste the inside of my mouth. The best thing my mother cooked was beef stew. If she put carrots in it, George Senseney had a temper tantrum. I was always afraid that he would hit my mother. As far as I can remember, he never did, but he certainly wanted to. "Just pick the carrots out," my mother said in a voice that muffled scorn.

George's anger came on in an instant. His face, usually so cheerful and friendly, would darken, and the skin around his mouth tightened. One night we were eating in the kitchen and he threw a Portuguese ceramic bowl against the wall. Salad fell all over the floor. The sound of the bowl shattering made me think all the light in the world was going out and I was going to die. The most peaceful meal was breakfast. Our mother put five or six boxes of dry cereal in the middle of the kitchen table. Rice Krispies was my favorite because of the *snap*, *crackle*, and *pop* noises it made when you added milk and sugar. Blair and I each made a wall out of cereal boxes so as to hide our cereal bowls. Then we ate as slowly as we could and whoever finished last would say, "Now I can just enjoy mine!" Blair and I had some real fights about food. Both of us were overweight. We were greedy, like baby birds with beaks open.

Our mother took us on visits to her friends, mostly in the city, but sometimes we stayed overnight with people who had country houses. One of our mother's favorite places to visit was the writer Jeffrey Potter's basement apartment a few blocks from 124 East Eighty-Fifth Street. He was ten years younger than my mother and at least as handsome as my father, maybe even handsomer in a movie star way. What I liked about Jeffrey was that there was no difference between the way he talked to children and the way he talked to adults. He had a parrot that sat on his shoulder and said, "Polly wants a cracker!" I was allowed to feed the parrot pieces of cracker. Jeffrey was having an affair with my mother, but I didn't know. When I was in my twenties, he told me that the only time my mother had an orgasm during intercourse was when, during a dinner party, she made love with him under a glass table. I wished that Jeffrey had not told me this. I am not sure I believe it anyway. My mother relished her own hauteur and rarely let down her mask of reserve. My father enjoyed telling about the time he came to see my mother at Eighty-Fifth Street and discovered that Jeffrey Potter was hiding in a closet. My mother had feared that it was George Senseney whom she had heard climbing the stairs. Both men made a hasty exit.

Jeffrey's older brother, an alcoholic painter named Fuller, was an even better friend. He and his wife, Cindy, had two children, Benny, who was one of two Dalton boys I had a crush on, and Mary Barton, who was, for all the years I lived in New York, my closest friend. In 1950, Fuller Potter became a drinking companion of Jackson Pollock and, inspired by Pollock, he turned to action painting, went to Mexico, and brushed wild strokes of paint onto *petates* (straw mats) instead of onto canvas.

The Potters lived in a ground floor apartment a few blocks east of us in a neighborhood that was a little bit slummy. Benny had friends from nearby buildings with whom he made carts out of wood attached to roller skate wheels. Mary Barton was feisty: she made the boys give us turns. There were almost no cars, and if one came by, we just drove our carts over to the curb. Mary Barton taught me hopscotch and how to jump rope. Thin, small, and agile, she could do double Dutch. When I tried, the rope got tangled around my legs, and I prayed that Benny and his friends wouldn't see how clumsy I was.

I spent a lot of nights at the Potters' apartment. Benny would turn the radio on to crime stories, and he and Mary Barton and I would lie on our stomachs in a big bed listening to the *clunk*, *clunk*, *clunk* of footsteps as a murderer approached a victim. I had to block my ears. Mary Barton pretended to be terrified, just for fun. Lying near Benny was exciting. I held in my stomach when he was around, but I do not think that he noticed I was there.

The friends that my mother saw most often were Zizi Sversky and his two "wives," Moute and Colette, both French and, I think, sisters. They lived next door in a building about eight feet from my

Fuller Potter, c. 1952

bedroom window. Zizi played the piano and held musical evenings to which our mother sometimes took Blair and me. When we entered Zizi's apartment, he would kiss our mother on both cheeks and exclaim "Oh my beautiful Ondine!" My mother loved being called Ondine. She thought of herself as some kind of nymph or goddess. During these evenings, there was nothing to do and nothing to eat. I had to sit in one of the straight-backed chairs set out in two rows and not wiggle or make noise. To relieve my boredom, I focused my eyes on one small thing and then on another. It might be the corner of a Persian rug, the spout of a samovar, or the shine on wineglasses. Each detail was packed with mystery.

When George went to Zizi's with my mother and Blair and I stayed home, they didn't get a babysitter. After all, I could look out my bedroom window and see into Zizi's kitchen window. In fact, my mother never hired babysitters. I guess she trusted Blair and me not to get into trouble. It was fine if she was at Zizi's, but when she went other places I was scared. The five flights of stairs that led to our apartment were full of danger. A burglar could come down or up the fire escape and climb in through the kitchen window, or he could climb the alley wall and break my bedroom window. Alone in my bed, I would listen. Any noise sounded like a murderer's approach. I didn't dare move for fear that the rustle of bedcovers would give away my whereabouts.

It was not just murderers and burglars that scared me. It was wolves, packs of wolves that could rush out from under my bed. Sometimes, in order to get into the hall, I climbed from the top of one piece of furniture to the next without touching the floor. If I put my foot on the floor, the wolves would grab my ankle. Blair was afraid of wolves, too, especially the wolves under our claw-foot bathtub. When those wolves threatened to rush out at us, we would climb from the bathtub to the top of the sink, then onto the toilet from which we could leap out into the hall. One night when my mother and George were out, my crib broke. I do not know why I was still sleeping in a crib. Maybe there wasn't enough money to buy a bed. I must have been too heavy for the crib, because one end of the metal frame that held up my mattress fell to the floor and my mattress became a ramp with a pack of wolves rushing up to kill me. I got out of the crib, ran down the hall, and tried to open Blair's door. It wouldn't open so I screamed for her to let me in. No answer. I could not believe that my sister kept me out when wolves were about a foot away, panting with their shiny wet tongues hanging out over their teeth.

One way to avoid being scared was not to stay in bed. When my mother and George went out, Blair and I got up and played in the hall, which was so narrow that we could climb its walls by putting one foot and one hand on each wall. Our favorite game was called Wump. George taught it to us. We each covered ourselves with a blanket and, starting at opposite ends of the long hall, we crawled toward each other saying, "Wump! Wump!" When we bumped into each other, we pushed and pushed, blind as moles. Another game was tickling each other's backs. We made up stories to go with the tickling—a princess walking in the woods in search of something, or maybe our fingers traced the path of a mother rabbit and her bunnies investigating a vegetable garden. The imaginary footsteps made the tickle. Sometimes we lay on the bed they bought for me after my crib broke. If we laughed hard enough with our heads hanging near the floor, we thought we would fly.

George taught us other games as well. Maybe he liked playing with us because he rarely got to see his teenage son, Conrad, who went to the Kent boarding school in Connecticut. Also, our mother hated games. She only liked to read. In one game George taught us, one person drags her index finger in circles around the other person's palm, while saying, "Round and round the garden goes the teddy bear." Then she walks her fingers up the arm and into the armpit, saying: "Step, step, step, step, and tickle you under there!" In another game George cut a row of sharp teeth out of a piece of white paper, stuck it under his upper lip and chased us down the hall growling like a wolf. Blair and I each tried to get ahead so that we would not be eaten first.

Once when they came home from a party, our mother and George caught Blair and me playing in the hall. George warned us that the next time they went out he would put a piece of Scotch tape on both our doors. If the tapes came loose, he would know that we had left our rooms. Blair and I hatched a plan: I was to climb on my bureau and jump out of the little window that led from my bedroom to the hall. Blair would meet me there. Later I could re-stick the tape on Blair's door and climb back into my room through the window. The problem was that I was too small to reach the window from the hall floor. When they came home and George saw me rushing to my room, he stood in the doorway blocking my mother's view and giving me time to vanish. George was on my side, I thought.

George Senseney was, like all of my mother's husbands except the fifth one, tall, dark, and handsome. The aura of power and danger around him was magnetic. Blair and I liked him except when he was mad at our mother. This was usually in the evening after he'd had cocktails and then wine at dinner. I didn't know it then, but George was an alcoholic. He almost never got mad at Blair and me. He was fond of us, actually too fond. Asked what it was like to live with Lybie, he told a close friend of my mother's, the photographer Hans Namuth, that Lybie was wonderful, but the little girls were fantastic.

George was much more affectionate than our mother. When he said good night, he wasn't in a rush the way she was. He talked to us and he kissed us and tickled our backs, but then he went too far. Blair and I had separate bedrooms, so I did not know what happened to her until we were grown up. With me he would tickle my back and then his hand would travel slowly toward my vagina. He would caress me between my labia. I didn't ask him to stop. I liked the feeling. I had an inkling that it was naughty, but I wasn't sure it was abnormal. I had no idea what was or was not normal. With Blair, he went further. He took her to his and our mother's bed and tickled her back. Then he said that she must keep her part of the bargain. He made her masturbate him until he ejaculated into her hands. With her hands cupped, she walked down the long hall to the bathroom to wash off the goo. He told her not to tell our mother. He probably told me that, too, but I don't remember.

Photographs of Blair between eight and ten years old show an anxious girl, very beautiful like our mother, but with a sadness that was not childlike. At school, she behaved in such a nervous way that she had to go home after only a half day. She had tunnel vision (said to be a hysterical reaction). She would be looking at something and the center of what she was looking at would vanish. She remembers

Blair, c. 1945

Blair, c. 1946, Central Park,
New York City

being deaf, too. And she had a twitch. Her twitch consisted of moving her jaw back and forth. She was actually trying to wiggle her nose because her nostrils itched, and she was trying to press one side of a nostril against the other. (Blair was obsessed with noses— she had to touch them. She would suddenly reach up and squeeze a person's nose.) I thought the way she moved her jaw back and forth was glamorous, so for a while I copied Blair's twitch.

Dalton was concerned about Blair: she was sent to a woman psychiatrist who showed her some naked dolls. When Blair knew all about what a penis was, the doctor asked her how she knew. Blair said she saw her stepfather naked. The doctor asked her if anyone was touching her down there. "No," Blair answered quickly, "but, yes. Only once. My stepfather. But don't tell my mother." I do not know whether the psychiatrist told our mother. Perhaps she did, because Blair never saw that doctor again. If she had been told, our mother would have refused to believe it. When in my thirties, I told our mother what George had done, she denied it. She looked angry and changed the subject. Another time when I brought it up, she scoffed: "Oh, that kind of thing happens to everybody. It happened to me with my father."

During the years he was married to my mother, George drank more and more. The tissue paper butterfly over my mother and George's bed became a symbol of violence. Their bed was a place to avoid.

8

Granny Blair

Our mother often took us to 226 East Seventieth Street where her parents lived in a small two-bedroom apartment whose walls were brown because my grandmother was a manic depressive and she was too anxious to allow house painters into her home. Granny was heavy. Her face was gray, and she always wore black. She may have had only one dress, because parts of the cloth had lost some of its blackness and were shiny. Granny and Granddaddy didn't get up from their chairs when we arrived. I had to go over and give them each a kiss on the cheek, which I didn't feel like

Granny on our Cape Cod
beach, c. 1937

Granddaddy (Charles Hildreth Blair), 1940s

doing. But once I was sitting down and drinking a glass of ginger ale, I was happy. Granny always sat with her back to the window. Granddaddy sat on the right side of the sofa. Behind him hung a huge dark painting said to be by Claude Lorrain. Granddaddy had a round, pink face. He was fat, too, but his stomach made him look jolly. He usually wore three-piece suits, and when I sat on his lap and fished inside his vest for his watch chain, I felt how firm his chest was, whereas Granny's saggy belly rested on her thighs. Granddaddy's pocket watch was a marvel of intricacy. He showed me how to open it up to see the little wheels ticking inside.

Granddaddy always had a martini in his hand or on the cocktail table in front of him. He hardly talked—Granny talked a lot, especially when she was manic. When he picked up his martini glass, he would hold it out toward me and say, "Here's how!" That must have been what he said when he drank with friends at the Cornell Club. At his club, he was admired. Since Granny seemed not to notice that he existed, he probably needed adulation. He had once been rich with a seat on the New York Stock Exchange, but he lost all his money during the Depression, and Freddy Sheffield, my mother's sister Carolyn's husband, had to support both him and Granny. At the Cornell

Club Granddaddy found respect in part because his grandfather, Ezra Cornell had founded Cornell University. In Ezra Cornell's family photograph album, there are photographs of Ezra's wife and two daughters. Emma, Granddaddy's mother, was her father's favorite and he taught her Greek and Latin. But she was a depressive, and when she had children she couldn't look after them, so her older sister, Mary, took on the job. Emma's eyes haunted me. In photographs they look shadowy, so totally sad. Of course, Granny could not have inherited depression from her husband's mother, but she had some unhappy sisters of her own. On the North Shore of Maryland, the Belle sisters were noted beauties and they all married the right kind of men, but, those men, too, lost their fortunes after the 1929 Crash, and my mother told me that two of Granny's sisters committed suicide.

When Granny was not depressed, I sometimes spent the night in her little guest room. Blair did this more often than me because she was Granny's favorite. Granny gave Blair a big antique doll called Betty who had eyes that opened and real eyelashes. I longed

Ezra Cornell's wife Mary (center) with her
daughters Emma (left) and Mary (right)

to pick up Betty, but it was forbidden. I was given a less breakable doll, a baby with rubbery arms and a torso made of stuffed cotton cloth. During her manic phases, as a treat, Granny picked up Blair and me at Eighty-Fifth Street and took us to a hamburger place called Prexy's or sometimes to Hamburger Heaven, which I liked better because it had chairs that you climbed up into and then closed yourself in by pulling a hinged wooden tray/table toward you. The waiters placed our hamburgers and drinks right on this tray. When we crossed the street with Granny, she held my hand so tightly that it hurt. She was afraid that I would get run over. I was afraid to pull my hand away. I did not want to hurt her feelings.

Sometimes Granny came to our apartment bringing dresses with matching bloomers for Blair and me. She had made them herself out of seersucker printed with wild patterns. Because they were seersucker, our mother wouldn't have to iron. Most of my clothes were hand-me-downs from Blair, so a new Granny dress was exciting. One of my hand-me-down dresses was embroidered all around the skirt with swings upon which sat small brown bears made of fake fur. The bears swung when I walked. This was the dress I wore to birthday parties.

Granny and my mother and father with Hamlet, c. 1937

9

Birthday Parties

Some Dalton children had parents with a lot of money, and their birthday parties were elaborate with candied apples and a magician or a clown. We dunked for apples floating in a huge metal tub. You had to grab an apple with your teeth, no easy feat because the apples bobbed and rolled in the water and your face got all wet. My classmates had fantastic cakes, specially ordered from a bakery with their name and Happy Birthday written in pink icing across the top.

The problem was that my mother didn't understand the kinds of presents that were expected at Dalton birthday parties. Most people brought well-wrapped boxes that contained some new game or at least a book. My mother thought expensive presents were vulgar. Also, she didn't have much money because George Senseney was supporting her, and he didn't earn much. On the way to one party, my mother bought a pink helium balloon for me to give to the birthday girl. I was mortified. A balloon is something that you buy on your way home from the zoo. I was scared to enter the party with just a balloon, but I was lucky: the room was so crowded that nobody noticed.

My birthday parties were simple. My mother painted a donkey on a big sheet of brown wrapping paper, cut it out minus the tail, and hung it on a wall. We each had a turn to be blindfolded, turned around three times, and given a paper tail to pin on the donkey's rump. We also played blind man's buff and musical chairs, for which my mother arranged two rows of chairs back-to-back, and we all walked around the chairs while she played music on the phonograph. When the music stopped, we rushed to find a chair and sit down. There was always one less chair than there were players, so somebody was always out. Finally, there were only two people walking around one chair. The winner was the one who sat in it first. I didn't want to be out, but I really didn't want to be the winner sitting all alone on a single chair. The nicest part of a birthday was when my mother came into my room and said good night. She would lean down and give me a real hug and kiss. On her way out the door, she would turn and say, "Good night, birthday girl." A birthday girl was lovable.

Blair's birthdays were more fun than mine. For Blair's tenth birthday party our mother brought a container of dry ice to Central Park and we all got to throw a piece of ice into a stream and watch it smoke and sizzle. Blair invited three girls and four boys, all Dalton friends. My favorite boys were Benny Potter and Johnny Myers. At Valentine's Day at Dalton, the teachers placed a big cardboard box with a slit in the top in the school lobby and you could slide valentines into it. I made valentines for Benny and Johnny, but I didn't write my name on them. I didn't want them to know I had crushes on them. At Blair's birthday picnic I watched Benny and Johnny without letting them see that I was looking at them.

Except when we first arrived in New York and she left us with Ellie, my mother was not a big present giver. For one birthday, she gave me a thick book called *The Jumbo Fun Book*. It was full of games and poems and things to do. That was where I found the only poem that I could memorize, a poem that made me first sad and then happy. Blair and I made up gestures to go with it and we recited it together:

> *There once was a puffin just the shape of a muffin,*
> *and he lived on an island in the great blue sea,*
> *and he ate little fishes which were most delicious,*
> *and he had them for breakfast and he had them for tea.*

But this poor little puffin, he couldn't play nothin'
'cause he hadn't anybody to play with at all.
So, he sat on his island and he cried for a while,
and he felt very lonely and he felt very small.
Then along came the fishes and they said if your wish is,
you can have us for playmates instead of for tea,
so they all play together in all sorts of weather,
and the puffin eats pancakes like you and like me.

My mother gave me other books, too. Wanda Gag's *Millions of Cats*, *The Story of Ferdinand*, *The Little House*, *The Runaway Bunny*, *Br'er Rabbit*, *Alice in Wonderland*, *D'Aulaires' Book of Greek Myths*, *The Water Babies*, *Winnie-the-Pooh*, *Stuart Little*, and a wonderful book called *Poo-Poo and the Dragons*, which had a dramatic picture of a dragon going under a bridge and humping his back until the bridge fell down. Of course, we had Grimm's Fairy Tales, Beatrix Potter books, and a book of Mother Goose nursery rhymes. I loved

Me age four, summer 1945

rhymes. They made the world seem a place where everything fit neatly together. Nothing would fall apart. Lying in bed at night I invented a poem that began: "Rabbits, rabbits, brown and white. Tell your babies to be polite." My verse made me proud. I day-dreamed that I might be a poet.

Another present from my mother was roller skates. At first, she held my hand. She wasn't a person who liked to touch, so holding my hand was not something she did often. It felt awkward, but I liked it. Skating down the sidewalk on the park side of Fifth Avenue was exhilarating, especially because the sidewalk was made up of hexagonal paving stones whose multitude of cracks created a *clickety-clack* noise as my skates rolled over them. I decided that these cracks were not dangerous. They would not break my mother's back. Often I went home with a bruised knee, but I didn't care. Blair never fell. She was better than me at everything.

10

Thoughts

Imust have been four years old when I was walking down the long, narrow hall at Eighty-Fifth Street and I suddenly realized that other people had thoughts and feelings tossing around inside their heads. This was a comfort. I had worried that I was the only one. Now I knew that everyone was like me, even Blair, even my mother. I looked at their heads and I knew their secret—they had ideas inside. I wondered what kind of thought Blair was having. Her face never told me. I would never be able to see what she was thinking.

The world at age three or four or even five is an unstable place. Gravity cannot be trusted. Indoors and outdoors are either all one thing or they are totally separate. My room and out of my room could be different realities. I began to think that the life Blair and I were living every day was just one life and that it might be going on inside another world, which might be inside yet another world. It was like one reel of film turning and turning inside another reel whose happenings we could neither see nor hear. If I could break through to that other reel, who would I find living there, what would they be doing, and would I land in a different piece of time? Outside of that reel there might be more reels. It could be worlds within worlds within worlds, and so on forever. I wished that I believed in God. God could be in charge of everything.

Some nights I would lie in bed worrying about death. My mother had told me that, like my dead turtle, I would have to die.

When I had the giggles and wanted them to stop, I thought of the saddest thing I could think of: "My father is dead." I was afraid that my mother might die, too. Once I saw her fall down the stairs backward. It might have been a dream, but I can still see the exact look of terror on her face. It shocked me because my mother was never afraid.

There were songs we sang and games we played that made me think of death. "Ring-a-round the rosie, A pocket full of posies, Ashes! Ashes! We all fall down." We sang this while dancing in a circle, then we fell on the floor pretending to be dead. I figured that if I lived to be old, I had a lot of years left, but still, the end of living scared me. It was much worse than thinking about the time before I was born when Blair and my parents were together doing things every day. That they might keep on talking and eating and laughing even if I was dead was chilling. The thought that my dead body would fertilize a tree gave no comfort. I pictured red and yellow tulips on my grave. That didn't help either: I would not be able to see them. Seeing was the most important part of living. I had heard of heaven and God and angels in the sky. It was fun to think of someday cavorting with them on top of clouds. But I couldn't believe in an afterlife. My mother was an atheist. After death, there was nothing.

Besides death I had two other big worries—infinite time and endless space. The idea of time passing forever meant that if time were broken up again and again into incredibly minute bits, there would be no such thing as an instant, and you would hardly exist. There was nothing but time in front and time behind, nothing in between. And even if you did exist in an infinitesimal grain of time, the faster time swept toward you and vanished behind you, the closer you were to death. But once I had experienced how long a year was—getting through winter, spring, summer, fall, having another birthday, and moving from one grade to the next—I was less anxious about dying. The vastness of space, the idea that emptiness went on endlessly—that was still fearsome. Lying in bed I looked up at my ceiling and saw in my mind that at the top of the sky the universe was enclosed by an immense dome made of bricks. There could be more blue sky on the other side, but I didn't want to think about that.

11

The City

Our mother liked to explore different parts of the city. No matter what we did with her, she always made it seem as though no one had ever done such a thing before. Every month or so we would take the subway down to Chinatown, and I would struggle to eat with chopsticks at whichever restaurant our mother decided must be good because it was crowded with Chinese people. The Chinese people looked well fed, which surprised me, because whenever Blair and I did not want to eat Brussels sprouts, our mother would say, "Think of the poor starving Chinese!" I imagined digging a hole so deep that I would come out in China. In a picture book there was a Chinese girl with a pigtail and a round face like mine. She lived in a green valley surrounded by rice paddies. I wished that I could crawl through the tunnel I had dug and, just for a day, I could be her friend.

After lunch we wandered through the streets, ducking in and out of shops that sold Chinese novelties like paper dragons whose tails and heads were attached to sticks. When you pulled the sticks apart the dragon became long and colorful. My favorite thing to buy was a closed clamshell that I took home and put in a glass of water. In a few hours, it opened up and paper flowers grew out of it. A miracle. In my room, I had other more permanent toys—marbles, jacks, a spinning top, a hobby horse, and my fuzzy animals: Dumbo, the squishy elephant, and Buttoneyes, my brown musical bear that my father's mother gave me.

On Easter, we always went to Harlem. The children in the Easter parade had such enviable party dresses with lots of tulle, ribbons, and ruffles. The women wore fantastic hats—lavender, yellow, robin's-egg blue. Going to Harlem was like going to another country. I hoped that we blended in, but I don't think we did. My mother didn't mind at all.

Every week or so our mother took us to the Metropolitan Museum. She was good about it. Instead of heading straight up the wide marble staircase in order to look at European paintings, she took us first to the Egyptian section where we looked at mummies and tried to picture the dead body inside the wrappings of off-white strips of cloth. From there we went to see the room of Medieval armor with its enormous warrior on top of a gigantic horse. For all her effort to keep us interested, when my mother finally got to the rooms of nineteenth-century French painting and stood for a long, long time in front of each Cézanne, I scuffed my shoes along the polished floor and acted as though I wasn't looking at anything.

Every year we went to the Barnum & Bailey Circus. Sometimes I got frantic. If I looked at the tightrope walker or the tiny car out of which countless clowns emerged, I would miss the elephants with their ponderous but eloquent walk. I was so slow at seeing things. Blair could watch all three rings at once. Our mother bought us each a toy that consisted of a circle of tin painted red and blue and attached to a handle. When you pumped a lever on the handle the circular shape whirled around like a windmill and made sparks.

One year I got to go to the ballet twice. I had already been to a ballet with my mother when, one night, she woke me up and told me to quickly get dressed. Fuller Potter had an extra ticket for *Swan Lake*, my favorite ballet. I sat next to Mary Barton, but for once we didn't talk. Both of us were fixated on the swan. I followed the swan's movements with my own muscles. I leapt and spun and pointed my toe toward the sky. I felt tall, thin, and beautiful. Leaving the theater, I walked with my toes pointing outward. I wondered if anyone noticed that there was a ballet dancer inside of me.

Our mother never worried that something bad might happen to Blair and me. We were allowed to go out when it was already dark and walk a block and a half to the stationary store at the corner of Eighty-Fourth Street and Lexington. Here, with money that George or our mother gave us or that came from the tooth fairy, we bought candy, Neccos for me and for Blair, who had grown-up taste in foods, licorice. If we had enough money, we bought trading cards. With friends I traded away my boring cards or the cards for which I had duplicates for cards I didn't have. The most popular cards were called Pinkie and Bluey. Pinkie is a 1794 portrait by Thomas Lawrence of an eleven-year-old girl with a pink sash. Bluey is Thomas Gainsborough's 1776 *The Blue Boy*, a portrait of a handsome young man dressed in blue satin. The next most sought-after cards had images of famous racehorses.

Before Blair and I left the stationary store, we checked out the latest comics. One time I really wanted a paperback joke book, but I didn't have enough money, so I just took it and walked out. Blair and I were halfway back to Eighty-Fifth Street when we heard the store owner coming after us. I threw the joke book into a dark doorway. When the store owner reached us, my hands were empty. After he returned to his store, I grabbed the book and we ran home.

After that, I decided that stealing was too dangerous. The only other time I stole something was from a friend of my mother's, Lotti Bruel. In her house in Cornwall, Connecticut, she had a tiny ashtray decorated with many different colors of enamel. It was so beautiful. I knew my mother would like it, so I put it in my pocket and took it home. My mother told me it was wrong to take other people's things, and she made me give it back. I had to walk through the swampy woods to Lotti's house all alone, trying not to think of the wolf in "Little Red Riding Hood." As long as you look straight ahead and never look behind bushes to see what's lurking there, you can refuse to be afraid. When Lotti came to the door, I quickly handed her the ashtray, said I was sorry, and raced out into the pine trees where no one could see me.

My mother rarely got angry. I do not think that she paid close enough attention to get mad, but one day Blair told a lie and our mother was furious. I was scared and sad for Blair, but at the same time sort of glad. Probably Blair had said that she hadn't done some bad thing that she actually had done. Quite often Blair blamed me for things. As I listened to our mother's harsh words, I decided to be a good girl and never to lie. For a little while after this I believed that my mother loved me best.

Perhaps the amount of freedom our mother gave us was not unusual in the 1940s. Still, I wonder about her letting Blair and me go to the movies alone on weekends. She would drop us at the Trans-Lux movie theater, which I remember being on the southwest corner of Eighty-Fifth Street and Madison Avenue. This was a huge treat, but I suspect it was a way of getting rid of us for a couple of hours. Before the movie began, there were newsreels about the war. After the newsreels, there was always the same brief film about soldiers raising the American flag on a flagpole on top of a small hill. The audience would stand and sing "The Star-Spangled Banner." Next came previews. In one of them I saw a man wearing dark clothes and black gloves walk into a park and squat behind a bench. Scary music warned me that something bad was about to happen. It did. Another man came and sat on the bench and a minute later two gloved hands came up from behind the bench and strangled him. After seeing this preview, I always slept with my sheets and blankets pulled up over my neck.

Another thing that our mother let us do was to go to Central Park alone. Most often we went to the Eighty-Fifth Street playground just two and a half blocks away. But late one afternoon

Blair and I decided to go to Mother Goose playground. We had to go down Fifth Avenue to Seventy-Second Street and then walk through Central Park until we came to an oval fence made of tall black metal bars. Usually this playground was full of uniformed nannies and well-dressed children, but when Blair and I visited, it was empty except for a woman with a baby carriage who was getting ready to leave. Something was wrong. A playground with no children feels desolate. Even the statue of Mother Goose riding a goose at the playground's far end looked forlorn, and the swings made long black shadows on the pavement.

Having come all this way, Blair and I thought we had better have a little fun. We spent a few moments on the seesaw. Because Blair weighed so much more than me, she had to sit halfway up her side of the seesaw. I was always afraid that she would get off without warning me and I would go crashing to the ground. This had happened a few times. It didn't really hurt, but I hated the surprise.

The jungle gym was my favorite. I could do somersaults at the bottom—once I chipped my front tooth doing that. Climbing to the top made me feel nimble and courageous. I got there before Blair, and I looked down and sang the words that she liked to sing to me: "I'm the king of the castle, and you're the dirty rascal!" I was up there feeling regal when I noticed a man outside the playground holding on to the fence bars and watching me. "Ah," he said. "I see you can climb all the way to the top!" I was enjoying his admiration of my climbing prowess when I heard Blair's urgent voice saying, "Hayden, come down immediately!" I refused to relinquish my power. Instead I watched the man as he moved sideways, always facing me. It was getting dark. His hands went slowly from bar to bar as if he didn't want Blair and me to notice that he was moving toward the playground entrance. Blair stood at the bottom of the jungle gym shouting for me to come down. Finally, I heard the fear in her voice, and I realized that the man was a kidnapper. I climbed down and ran behind Blair to the exit. We got there just before the man did and we kept running all the way out of the park and across Fifth Avenue. It was a relief to hide in a group of people waiting for the uptown bus. My heart was beating so fast I couldn't talk. Blair had saved us. How lucky I was to have an older sister. When we got home and told our mother that we were almost kidnapped, she was unimpressed. Her unconcern made me feel silly. Maybe we just invented that he was a kidnapper. But I could tell from Blair's solemn face that we had been in danger and that our mother either refused to believe it or she didn't care.

Me and Blair,
Central Park, c. 1946

12

Cornwall

George and my mother's friends, poet and playwright Montgomery (Monty) Hare and his wife, May, gave us permission to build a log cabin on their land in Cornwall, Connecticut. The piece of land my mother and George chose was about a ten-minute walk from the Hares' house. You went past the Hares' swimming hole, up along a ridge, and through a pine forest to a clearing in the woods. When the cabin was ready, we spent every weekend there.

It must have been before the cabin was built that we camped in two tents near the future cabin's site. After eating supper cooked on a camp stove, my mother put Blair and me to bed. In the middle of the night I woke up to find myself alone. I called out. No one answered. To keep bears and murderers away, I made sure that the sides of the tent touched the ground. I stayed completely still so as not to alert killers to my presence. At last a flashlight beam shone through the tent's green mosquito netting. I heard excited voices and I started to cry. My mother explained that the war was over and to celebrate, they had gone on a hayride. Blair told me that there were lots of nice boys in the hay. There was singing and fireworks and doughnuts to eat. I was envious and angry. How could they have left me alone at night in the forest? My mother kept saying how wonderful it was that the war was over. I was too young to go on a hayride, she said. There were no other four-year-olds there.

The log cabin that George built had one big room. Just off the living room there was a tiny alcove with bunk beds for Blair and

Me, Cornwall, CT, 1946

me. The kitchen was part of the living room. All it had was a kero-
sene stove and a sink with a hand pump to draw water. My mother
and George slept in the living room in a double bed covered with a
soft Indian print bedspread. With bolsters placed against the wall,
the bed also served as a sofa. There was no bathroom. We brushed
our teeth in the kitchen sink, bathed in the Hares's pond, and went
outside to use a chemical toilet.

In Cornwall, when he said good night, George was affectionate,
but since Blair and I were in the same room, he didn't do anything
more than tickle our backs. Before we went to sleep, Blair and I
would tell ghost stories and play games that George taught us. One
game was to squeeze your sister's hand three times. That meant "I
love you." I was on the top bunk so I would hang my arm over the
edge of my bed, and Blair would reach up. The second person answered with two squeezes meaning "How much?" The first person
squeezed as hard as possible, meaning, "a lot." I always squeezed
as hard as I could, but I didn't want it to hurt. A similar game consisted of knocking on the pine wall three times—"I love you." The

other person answered with four knocks—"I love you, too." This I love you game would go on and on until we were too sleepy to knock. If I was the first one to stop knocking, I felt guilty. I wanted Blair to know that my love for her was bigger than a mountain.

George made us a swing. He tied it to a high branch of a tree on the side of a hill so that once you got going, pumping as hard as you could, the swing would fly way out high above the ground. Sometimes I went so high that I was afraid the swing would keep going up and it would sail all the way around. Of course, that never happened. Blair liked me to do "run-unders," which consisted of pushing Blair until she went high enough for me to run out under the swing without her legs bumping into my head. We also twisted the swing around and around and then let go and the swinger would whirl in circles, get dizzy, and fall off. The ground beneath the swing was full of wild strawberries. When we were tired of swinging, we sat on the ground and ate them.

George acquired an army hammock. It was khaki green with a canvas roof and side walls with khaki green mosquito netting windows. He hung it in the woods about two hundred feet from our cabin. Blair and I sometimes spent nights there. It could be frightening because of wild animals, but we had flashlights and if we got

A friend, Blair, and me in Hare's pond,
Cornwall, c.1946

too scared, we could run back to the log cabin. George even made us a tree house on top of a pine tree with lower branches that were easy to climb. I went there to pretend that I was alone in the world. Nobody could get at me. I could take care of myself.

The Hares' pond where we swam every day was full of polly-wogs and, near the shore, salamanders. We dumped our clothes on a stone wall, dragged inner tubes into the water, and floated with our bottoms under water. My mother had a favorite walk to a swimming place on the Housatonic River. We followed a narrow tar road past fields with cows. Normally I didn't like walking, but this walk was full of pleasures—the rich brown smell of cow patties, wild irises that grew up all on their own. And there were daisies, so many of them that it didn't matter if Blair and I picked a few and pulled their petals off one by one: "He loves me, he loves me not, he loves me, he loves me not . . ." If the last petal pulled was a "not," I was sad, even though I was vague about whether it was Benny Potter or Johnny Myers who did not love me.

In the opposite direction from the walk to the river was the walk to Lotti Bruel's house. Part of this walk went through a swamp. We had to jump from hummock to hummock to avoid getting our feet wet. Even after I stole Lotti's ashtray, she was kind to me. She baked German-style pastries and served them to us on little plates. We sat on her sofa and listened to the grown-ups talk. I didn't understand a word they said, but I enjoyed the rise and fall of voices. It was like being in bed and listening to adults in the next room. Every muscle in my body went slack. My mind went slack, too. On the way home Blair and I stopped at the edge of the swamp and dug in the mud to make islands and canals and castles—a city where fairies might live.

In Cornwall, I learned to ride a two-wheeled bicycle. Trying to keep up with Blair as we rode down a long, steep hill took all my courage. I was torn between wanting to dump my bike on the side of the road and wanting to coast downhill with the wind blowing my hair. George came home one day with a bright red three-wheeled motorcycle with a trunk on the back that had an arched chrome handle on either side. When he gave Blair and me rides, we yelped with joy and clung to each other while hanging tight onto those chrome handles. But after a while George went too fast and he didn't stick to the road. The forest floor was bumpy, and once when I was alone, I screamed for him to stop because I was too small to reach both handles at the same time. He acted as though he had not heard. Finally, he slammed on the brake and told me I could find my way home.

George had a pistol. He would go up to a clearing on a hill behind the cabin and practice shooting. I was impressed with his manliness, but the noise made me jump. Once George took me up to his shooting range and put the gun in my hands. It was cold and heavy. I didn't like the feel of it, so I gave it back to him. Blair told me that with her he had insisted that she shoot the pistol. He showed her how to aim and to pull the trigger. She was nine or ten years old. From then on, she and I did not like guns.

At night after supper we were allowed to read in the living room for a little while. We sat on the bed and pulled books down from the shelf that George had built above it. There were children's books, but I already knew all the stories, so I took down a fat grown-up's book and followed the lines of print with my finger. Almost every line had a word that I recognized—little words like "the" or "she." Mostly I looked at the shapes of words. I pretended that I was actually reading. During one of these quiet times my mother heard a strange noise outside the door. She looked out and there was a skunk looking at her just as if he were an expected guest. Instead of screaming or slamming the door, she said, "Good evening, Mr. Skunk. Please go away." And the skunk did.

Getting to Cornwall on Friday afternoons was sometimes by car with our mother and George and sometimes alone by train.

Whoever it was that put Blair and me on the train at Grand Central Terminal would ask the conductor to keep an eye on us. The conductor gave us each a coloring book and a pack of Crayola crayons. When the train began to move, it felt as if the walls around the tracks under Grand Central were moving and we were staying still. When I pressed my nose to the window, my breath fogged the glass and I wrote my initials and then watched the letters fade. Then I drew hearts. Blair had just taught me how to draw them, first one side, then the other, so that the heart's two halves were equal. They faded, too. Riding out of Manhattan was always a shock. I looked into windows of apartment buildings where everything inside was gray or brown, even the people. They were poor. I was grateful that I did not live where they did.

About halfway through our train trip a man came down the aisle selling candy and cigarettes. Blair and I shared a Hershey bar. She handed me the half with no wrapping, so my fingers got all brown and I licked them almost clean, then quickly, so no one could see, I wiped my hands on the fuzzy velvet seat. Our mother picked us up at Cornwall Bridge and took us to the cabin. Driving back to New York on Sunday nights, I slept on the floor of our car and Blair slept on the seat. But when we started down the West Side Highway I woke up. George was driving so fast I was afraid he would plunge us into the river.

13

Dasya

The summers we spent with our father on Horseleech Pond were my favorite time of year, not just because of the pond, but also because I was a little bit in love with my father. During the school year I never knew where he was living or what he was doing. Seeing him again in June was exciting but also anxious-making. What if he didn't like me anymore? What if I looked too chubby? I wanted him to say how wonderful I was, but he never did. His mind was elsewhere. He would tease me and call me Hayden Wayden, but he didn't play with me. He was always worrying about his

Dasya Chaliapin at the Turkey Houses, 1947

properties—the army barracks houses and their tenants. He spent a lot of time fixing things up. He was good at repairs.

In the summer of 1947 I met my father's third wife, Dasya Chaliapin. And I met her son, Hugh Robertson, who was just my age (six). Hugh's father was a partner in Todd, Robertson and Todd, managing agents for John D. Rockefeller Jr. It was he who fired Diego Rivera in 1933 when Rivera had almost completed his Rockefeller Center mural into which he had inserted a portrait of Lenin. Dasya's Russian mother had persuaded her daughter not to fight for custody of Hugh, presumably because she considered Dasya to be an unfit mother or because she believed Hugh would lead a more privileged life with his wealthy American father. Dasya rarely saw her son, but Hugh was allowed to spend time with us during Turkey House summers.

Hugh was gentle and quiet, not like other boys. He quickly became my complete brother. When we were exploring the woods

Dasya's son, Hugh Robertson, and me at
Horseleech Pond, 1947

uphill from the turkey houses, we found a place beneath large oak trees where the ground was covered with bright green moss, the kind that if you pass your hand over it feels like mohair velvet. We made this place our hideout. Pushing dead leaves to either side, we cleared a path to the hideout through pitch pines and shrub oak. We tied strips torn from an old sheet on branches so as not to lose our way. I had thought of leaving pieces of bread like Hansel and Gretel, but I remembered that in that story, the birds ate the crusts and the children got lost and an old woman was going to roast them in her oven.

In the middle of the moss carpet we found a hollow at the base of the biggest oak tree. This was our secret hiding place. In it we stored candy and peanut butter and a few dimes—if something bad happened, these could be our emergency supplies. Hugh and I would sit and examine the minutia on the ground around us—tiny flowers growing in the moss, pine cones, acorns, pine needles. We tried to imagine a perimeter for our hideout, the line where walls would be if it had walls. The ground and the trees just went on and on, but we knew exactly where our hideout ended and where the forest began.

While he was married to Dasya, our father—usually not much of a present giver—gave Blair and me Russian shirts of heavy blue cloth with red and white embroidery around the neckline. Hugh already had one. I thought my new shirt made me look like a cute little Russian girl. I knew about Russia from a Russian folk tale told in a book called *My Mother Is the Most Beautiful Mother in the World*. My mother must have given it to me, or maybe Dasya did. Both of them felt beautiful. It was the story of a three-year-old Russian girl who lost track of her mother while farmworkers were harvesting wheat. The wheat fields were so high that the girl could not see over the top to find her mother. When she asked people if they had seen her mother and they asked who her mother was, she said, "My mother is the most beautiful woman in the world."

Finally, she found her mother, who turned out to be a plump and plain peasant woman.

I read this book over and over, in part because it showed me how much little girls love their mothers and how much they don't want to lose them, especially a beautiful mother like mine. But I loved this book also because I had a terror of getting lost. Even before getting lost on Lexington Avenue, I had been lost on Cape Cod. When I was two or three, my parents took me to their friend Jack Hall's house on Bound Brook Island on Wellfleet's bay side. Jack and his wife, Dodie, had a son named Darius who was born the same year as me. While the grown-ups drank cocktails, Darius and I went outside to play. We walked over a sandy hill carpeted with bearberry that in the 1940s, before the pitch pines took over, covered the hills and valleys of Bound Brook Island. Suddenly I found myself alone. Darius must have gone back over the hill to his home. Because of the hill the Halls' house was invisible. I couldn't remember the direction from which we had come. I found a dirt road and walked along it. It must lead someplace. After a while a Jeep came along, and the driver took me back to the Halls. My mother acted as though she had not noticed that I was gone, but Dodie knew. "There you are!" she said, as if my return was the best thing in the world.

Blair once went wandering off, too. Before I was born, Blair, aged two or three, was in a playpen made of chicken wire that our father had erected outside the Big House. Hamlet, our red setter, was in the pen with Blair and he decided to dig a hole under the chicken wire to get out. Blair crawled out after him and walked about a mile along a dirt road to the home of Anna Matson whose five-year-old son, Peter, Blair adored. When she got there, no one was home. It started raining, so she turned around and retraced her steps. Blair wasn't scared at all. She never thought that she was lost. In the meantime, our father telephoned the police and various friends to say that Blair was missing. Blair recalls that a truck came along—she thinks our father's friend Lloyd Rose, then a young art teacher (later a master chimney-maker and Truro Selectman) was at the wheel. Rose picked her up and took her home. All she remembers about that ride was the window wipers pushing rain off the windshield.

Dasya had the advantage of being thirteen years younger than my mother. She was plump with fair skin, big breasts, and soft, wavy, light brown hair. She loved to sing and play the accordion and to dance Russian dances. She taught us a Russian song, the words of which sounded like: "Cheesik, peesik, cadetskiville, nafontante . . ." That's all I remember. Dasya said the song was about a drunken canary.

Dasya liked to have fun. She had nothing of my mother's hauteur. My mother always looked as though no one could approach her. She fended off people with her exquisite jaw line, with the aquiline bridge of her nose, her narrow nostrils, and her pale blue eyes. She reminded me of the fairy-tale princess on top of the glass mountain whom no suitor could reach. My father told me that when my mother was married to him, she was shy and didn't talk much. She liked to be still, to look mysterious and poetic, slightly melancholy like Greta Garbo. She had a bit of Marlene Dietrich's femme fatale attitude. My father was quiet and reserved, too, dignified without being cold. In spite of his humor and his elegant seductive manner, he was not entirely accessible. He was not cozy. Everyone remarked on his great charm, a charm that made people—especially his daughters—want to win his admiration. His understated wit was typically New England. Thoreau was his role model, maybe Emerson, as well. He liked to sit on a log in the middle of a forest. Being silent and observing nature was what made him happy.

Dasya, on the other hand, was wild and uninhibited. Everything about her radiated outward. She didn't take much in. Later I learned that she was an alcoholic. My father recalled his disdain when, during a period when it was hard to get meat because of the war, she ate two steaks all on her own.

Edmund Wilson noted in his diary a piece of gossip about my father and Dasya that Hayden Walling had just told him: "Story about Jack Phillips when he was married to Dasya Chlyapin[sic]: she wanted him to make love to her all the time and Jack had finally said there are other things to do besides making love. She had asked him what they were. Why, you can go fishing or take a walk. . . . Just to show you how cozy we are out here: Libby and her present husband (she had formerly been married to Jack) moved into Jack's house with him last summer, and my former wife was living with them, too."

Dasya had a July birthday. She was turning twenty-six. She told Blair and Hugh and me that it was a Russian tradition for children to decorate a birthday girl's chair with flowers. The yellow wicker chair that she chose was like a throne. It had a tall rounded back with elaborate floral designs woven into the wicker. The three of us set out in a search for flowers. The problem was that almost no flowers grow near Horseleech Pond. Perhaps we found honeysuckle, sweet pepperbush, goldenrod, or a bit of wild laurel. We wove leafy branches and whatever flowers we had been able to collect into the weave of the yellow chair. It was magnificent. It would make Dasya feel like a queen.

Just before the guests arrived Dasya came in dressed in a full peasant skirt, a wide black elastic belt, and a white, low-cut blouse. She had tied a narrow black velvet ribbon around her neck. She thanked us for the decorated chair and then, at the sound of car doors opening and closing, she went off to greet her guests. As she ushered them into the house, she asked Blair and Hugh and me to go outside. It's a grown-up party, she said. I was horrified. How could anyone be so mean, especially after we had worked so hard on her chair? We went behind the house and stood at the window

looking in. Dasya put Russian music on the Victrola and began to
dance, at first all by herself. Her full skirt went straight out, and
you could see her underpants. Her cleavage was more and more in
evidence because her blouse kept coming untucked and when she
tucked it back under her belt, her neckline got lower and lower.

Hugh's skinny shoulder was pressed against mine. I looked at
his sad face and asked him if he wanted to go to our hideout. He
did. We went and lay down on the moss. It was almost dark when
my father came to collect us. We went home for a quick supper (the
birthday cake was gone) and then to bed.

When Dasya and my father drove to Wellfleet to buy groceries
or to visit a friend, Hugh and Blair and I played a game we made
up. Blair and I were princesses who had fallen asleep by a magic
charm. Only a prince could wake us. We lay on the living room
floor with our legs slightly apart. Hugh would come and tickle our
arms and then our legs and finally he found his way to between
our legs. Hugh found the spot that could undo the spell and let the
princesses wake up. It was just a game; nevertheless, I would have
been ashamed if anybody found out.

My father once drove Hugh and me to Hugh's father's summer home in the fancy part of the Cape—I think it was Chatham
or Woods Hole. I hadn't realized that Hugh's visit to the Turkey
Houses was over until we got there. His father's house was called a
cottage, but it was huge, room after room full of antique furniture
and oval hooked rugs. Hugh took me up to his room, and we sat on
the bed and talked or tried to talk. Hugh was not crying. Like me
he was a holder-backer of tears. It was obvious that he didn't want
to be with his father. The house had a dark atmosphere. It had too
many unused rooms. Usually I liked visiting rich people's houses.
The Fifth Avenue apartment of my mother's younger sister, Aunt
Carolyn, was full of polished mahogany, upholstered furniture, and
heavy, lined curtains that pulled back with a string. Going there

made me feel grand. But the Robertsons' house had nothing fun in it.

When I was in my twenties, Anna Matson told me about Hugh turning up at her Cape Cod house. He had not been in these Wellfleet/Truro woods for over twenty years. Hugh asked Anna where his mother was. Anna did not know. I did, but I wasn't there to tell him. If Dasya was still alive, she was in France. In 1957, when I was going to school in Paris, my mother and I had Thanksgiving dinner at Dasya's home north of Paris. Now she had a jolly Russian husband, a drinker like herself. For the Thanksgiving feast she cooked two geese. The ballet dancer Serge Lifar was the only other guest. At lunch, he explained how he had avoided being arrested by the Nazis. He acted out his story with gestures, taking his penis out and demonstrating how he had shown the Nazis that he was not circumcised. Everyone at the table roared. I do not remember what Dasya said about what Hugh was doing at that time. Not long after visiting Anna in the 1960s, Hugh committed suicide.

14

Mougouch

In the autumn of 1948 my mother and father decided that it would be a good idea to join forces for a weekend in the Big House. He had separated from Dasya. They had not needed to get a divorce because, according to Massachusetts law, their marriage was not legitimate: when they married in 1946 they had not waited the required two years after my father's divorce from my mother. (They were three days short.) Now my father was in love with somebody else, a woman named Mougouch. I had just started third grade at Dalton. Blair was in sixth grade. In the last few months my mother and George had been fighting a lot. Given the friction between them and given the fact that George was a guest in my father's house, it was weird that over that weekend George seemed so relaxed. It was as if he owned the place.

My father came to the gathering at the Big House with his new love, Mougouch Gorky (née Agnes Magruder), and her two daughters, Maro, age five, and Natasha, age three. He had been introduced to Mougouch in late August at a party in New York given by Serge Chermayeff. Chermayeff took my father aside and told him to be nice to Mougouch. Her husband, the painter Arshile Gorky, had killed himself that July. My father and Mougouch were charmed by each other. He was a great dancer and so was she. Except for her slightly beak-like nose, she was beautiful. She had masses of brown hair and a mischievous twinkle in her blue-gray eyes. She and my father planned to meet again soon.

A few weeks after Chermayeff's party, my father was in Truro checking on his various rental properties. When he arrived at the Turkey Houses, he heard music. He went inside and there was Mougouch dancing with the Surrealist painter Roberto Matta Echaurren, who had been my father's Paper Palace tenant in 1942. That June 1948, Matta and Mougouch had had a brief affair. When Gorky found out, his jealousy was one of the torments that prompted him to hang himself. My father, always confidant about women, assumed that Mougouch was there on Horseleech Pond because she wanted to see him. He and Matta spent the rest of the afternoon vying for Mougouch's attention. My father must have won the battle, because a few months later, he and Mougouch and her daughters sailed for Spain.

Mougouch was, she told me later, horrified by the bizarre situation during that fall weekend in the Big House. Matta was still in her life, and George and my mother, though still married, were at odds. Blair and I were on our best behavior, hoping that our parents would fall in love again and remarry. I remember being asked

Mougouch in Orgeval, France, c. 1949

to take Maro and Natasha down to the shore of the pond. Maro was cantankerous. She came with me, but she made sure I noticed how reluctant she was. Looking back, her anger is not surprising: Gorky had died only two months earlier. By contrast, Natasha was scrumptious and sweet-tempered. She had dark corkscrew curls and she still had a bit of baby fat. Maro was skinny with a face that was beautiful but melancholy, the furthest thing from cute. She had olive skin and large brown eyes, and she looked like her Armenian grandmother, but I saw this resemblance only many years later. With the help of a lot of wine and bourbon, the adults managed to get through the weekend.

In October, after depositing Maro and Natasha in a Catholic school in Barcelona, my father and Mougouch looked all over Spain for an affordable place to live. Next, they searched for a home in Italy and settled in Positano for the winter, after which they decided to move to France. During this period, Matta was still in pursuit of Mougouch and she, ever restless and seeking adventure, traveled around Europe with one or the other of her two lovers. My father told me that once in Paris, after he and Mougouch quarreled, she jumped on a bus, and he, right in the middle of a boulevard, and with cars going by on either side, chased the bus and managed to jump on the back. "For a Bostonian," my mother once said, "your father was very passionate."

While carrying on this back-and-forth life, Mougouch installed Maro and Natasha in a Swiss boarding school, a deed for which Maro never forgave her mother. Natasha, who was only three, was spanked and shamed when she peed in her pants. She remembers being given a candy with a flower design in the middle as a reward on a day she didn't wet her bed. While being courted by my father and Matta, Mougouch got pregnant, she was not sure by who. She had an abortion. Perhaps that is why she placed her daughters in boarding school. Years later Mougouch insisted that she had camped in a tent near the school, thus, to her mind, she had not totally abandoned her daughters. Even so, her leaving such young children in Spanish and then Swiss boarding schools, like my mother's installing Blair and me in a Manhattan apartment with an Irish woman to look after us, might now seem horrifying to anyone for whom bringing up children was the central pleasure, duty, and purpose in life. Upper bohemian women like my mother and Mougouch defied the norms of decent behavior. They believed that there was a moral imperative to follow their desire.

Mougouch and my father finally settled in Orgeval, a town north of Paris. They got married in Paris by a justice of the peace at the Café de la Mairie in the Place Saint-Sulpice, and they held a reception at the Closerie des Lilas, a Left Bank restaurant frequented by artists and intellectuals. At this time, my father had a job as front man in the promotion of the Marshall Plan. With a diplomatic passport, he traveled all over Europe helping to organize traveling

Maro and Natasha in Europe, 1948

exhibitions that exalted the American way of life. The exhibitions moved through Europe in custom-built trailers whose sides folded down to form platforms with plexiglass walls. When my father got tired of being a sort of traveling salesman for American values, he was given a desk job in Paris, but this demanded being in an office and talking on the telephone, both of which he hated. The stammer that he had suffered in his youth returned, so he quit.

15

Hickory Ridge

My mother and George's fights became increasingly acrimonious. His rages made me wish I were invisible. The paper butterfly above their bed was a menace. The bed itself was a battlefield. George kept going out west on his secret missions. One day when he was away, our mother told Blair and me that we were going to go to a wonderful boarding school in Vermont. It was called Hickory Ridge and it was a feeder school for Putney, a progressive boarding school just a few miles away. Our mother made it sound like so much fun. There would be lots of nice children my age and there was a farm with animals to play with. She helped us pack a few clothes in a small duffle bag. The rest of our clothes she packed into a trunk to be shipped later. She took us to Grand Central and put us on an overnight train to Brattleboro, Vermont. She was going to Mexico to get a divorce.

I had the upper berth. We closed our heavy brown curtains that faced the aisle so that no one in the train's narrow corridor could see us. I left the curtain for the small window that faced outdoors open because I wanted to see what went by. Every time the train hooted, I looked out to see if there were lights from a town. With Blair on the berth below me I felt safe. The *clickety-clack* of the train's wheels lulled me to sleep.

The next morning when we stepped down from the train at Brattleboro, there was a man from Hickory Ridge to meet us. Fall term had begun a month earlier, so for the time being they put Blair and me in the same room. When our trunk arrived, the best things in it were two lavender taffeta duvets that our father's mother had given us. (We called them puffs.) At night Blair and I discovered that if we rubbed the corners of our puffs together sparks would fly. Competing to see who could make the most sparks, we shook our double decker bed so strenuously that after a couple of weeks it broke down and the school decided to separate us. Blair moved into a room with girls her own age and I moved into a room with a girl who was almost eight like me. Her name was Patsy Getz. Blair soon became one of the popular girls. At meals, she paid no attention to me. I felt abandoned.

A short walk from the school was a pond with a muddy bottom. I knew from turtle catching on Cape Cod that this was an ideal habitat for turtles. In the muck at the edge of the pond I found two small painted turtles. They had black backs with a little red at the edge. If you turned them over, the shell that shielded their tummies was yellow-orange. I always felt pity when I picked them up and they waved their legs with their tiny claws and then shut themselves inside their shells. But I wanted so much to have them. I carried the turtles back to my dormitory and put them in a bathtub that I thought no one ever used. With mud and grasses I built them a home. I was proud of my turtle house, but a few days later, the school's director came and remonstrated with me. She took me to the turtle's bathroom and asked, "Didn't you realize that the older girls need to use this tub?" She made me take the turtles back to the pond. I was shocked by her meanness. From then on, I hated this woman.

There was a girl at Hickory Ridge a year older than Blair called Aube Breton. She loved Blair, and I think she loved me, too. My mother or father must have asked Aube's mother, Jacqueline Lamba, to ask Aube to look after us. Jacqueline Lamba had left her husband, the Surrealist writer André Breton, and had gone off with

Monty Hare's brother, the sculptor David Hare. That must have been the reason she put Aube in this boarding school.

Aube was slender with a handsome, leonine face (like her father) and long, wavy light-brown hair. She was sure of herself and acted almost grown up, almost motherly. Like Blair and me, Aube wore full skirts and blouses that her mother bought for her in Mexico. Blair and I each had a red skirt with tiny flowers printed on it and a wide elasticized waist—good because we were overweight, and the waist could stretch to any size. After supper Aube and Blair and I often played records of classical music—Debussy's *Afternoon of the Faun* and Stravinsky's *The Firebird* and *The Rite of Spring*. We cleared a space in the dining room and danced around in bare feet. When the music got dramatic, we made dramatic gestures. Mostly I twirled. Twirling made me feel compact, all put together in one piece. Swimming did this, too. When you are dancing or swimming, air or water swirls around your body so that every part of your skin feels like one thing.

During morning assemblies at Hickory Ridge I learned a lot of songs. My favorites were "Flow Gently Sweet Afton" and "All

Me, Aube Breton, and three girls in Blair's class
at the Hickory Ridge School, 1948

Through the Night," gentle songs that I still associate with the view of long sunlit grasses on the hill outside the dining room widow. Aube taught us games, Surrealist games that she must have learned from her father. With Aube we made *cadavres esquisses*, a game in which each player draws a part of a figure starting with the head. The first player folds the paper so that the next player can see only the bottom lines of what she has drawn. The next player does the same thing. When we unfolded the paper, the resulting bodies were hilarious. Aube also taught us Truth, Consequences, or Over the Rooftop. If you were caught without your fingers crossed and someone said "Jinx!" you had to either answer any question with the truth or, if you chose consequences, you had to do whatever the person who said Jinx told you to do. This could be embarrassing, like having to kiss a boy. If you chose Over the Rooftop, you had to imagine that you were on a burning roof with two people that you loved. You could save only one person. It

Me in my Russian blouse,
Hickory Ridge School, 1948

was awful having to choose who to save and who to leave behind in the fire.

Schoolwork at Hickory Ridge wasn't too hard. For the first time in my life I was asked to write a story. I took it very seriously and was afraid it was no good, but the teacher liked it. Getting to the classroom building was a problem. I had a pain in the back of my ankles when I walked. Someone, maybe a doctor, told my parents it was because of short tendons. After that my father always teased me about my short tendons. Years later I learned that short tendons can be a tightening of the ankle tendon due to stress. Sometimes it hurt so much I could barely walk to class.

In my Hickory Ridge diary, I wrote, "Daddy is coming." A few pages later I wrote that he did not come. But in the middle of winter he did come. Blair and I had just learned to ski, and our father wanted to see us ski, so we started over to the ski hill. Walking on skis in deep snow, I fell and was so ashamed and angry that I just sat there. Blair and my father were far ahead of me. I lay down and put snow over my eyes to wash off tears. My father and Blair came back and stood over me. I refused to get up. He tried to cajole me by calling me "Hayden Wayden," but it felt insulting instead of loving. I wished I could melt away into nothing.

16

Toads

At the end of the school year, we went to Cape Cod. Since our father was in Europe, our mother, who was back from Mexico and now divorced from George, had persuaded him to let her use the Big House. Perhaps this was instead of child-care money. She planned to support herself by taking paying guests and by selling Mexican folk objects, silver jewelry, and indigenous clothing—embroidered blouses, long shawls, and serapes—to her upper bohemian friends.

A friend of my mother's named Stan Thayer helped with the paying guests. He was about thirty, had movie-star looks, and taught philosophy at Columbia University. Stan slept in one of two extra-long turkey brooder houses that my father had moved down from the dune and placed near where we parked our car. To make room for the paying guests, Blair and I moved out of the Big House and into the other brooder house. Our mother fixed it up with army cots and a big flashlight that she set on a wooden fruit crate. Every night when Stan Thayer put us to bed, he sat on a chair and told us long stories that he made up as he went along. We were spellbound. Before he left, he made sure that our flashlight worked and that we could reach it. Then he would kiss us good night just like a father.

We were alerted that some very rich New Yorkers were coming to stay. There was a flurry of tidying the house and making beds. These paying guests had a daughter my age. She was going to sleep in my vacated room. I thought it would be nice to welcome her with a gift of the tiny toads, no bigger than your thumbnail, that appear on the shore of Horseleech Pond in late summer. I loved to put them on the palm of my hand and feel the touch of their miniature feet as they hopped. Unlike turtles, who hate to be picked up, these toads were not afraid. They liked being with me, I thought. The afternoon before the rich people arrived, I collected maybe thirty toads in a basket and put them in the girl's room. I was sure that she had never seen such miniature toads and that she would be thrilled and would become my friend.

We could hear the New Yorker's car as it followed the long dirt road that leads to our house. A big black Buick descended the hill, so slowly—they must have been afraid of the bumps. My mother's eyes narrowed as she watched her paying guests getting out of the car. She scorned people with fancy automobiles. Buicks were vulgar, she said. I couldn't wait to see the girl's delight as she encountered my gift of toads. She and I would play with them and set them free. My mother ushered everyone to their bedrooms and when she came out of the girl's room, she was furious. The toads were lying all over the floor, dried up and dead. The girl's mother was horrified. It was like the turtles at Hickory Ridge: I was shocked that no one appreciated the sweetness of toads. My mother gave me a brush and a dustpan, and I swept up the toads and took them outside to a place under a tree where I covered them with leaves. It was my fault that they died. That paying guest girl did not become my friend.

Blair had friends her age and I did not. Her friends, Mary Day Lanier and Penny Jencks were usually nice to me—especially Penny. She included me in their play even though Blair would have preferred that I go away. We had a costume trunk and once, when Mary Day and Penny were at our house, we all dressed up in pink tulle ballet skirts and wreaths of flowers in our hair and we danced on the brick terrace. Blair took photographs. Mary Day, who already had breasts, wore no top and I wore no underpants so that my fat stomach was visible through the transparent skirt.

Penny often spent the night. When she was there, Blair didn't try to get rid of me. Penny would hide in a closet and then come out with her eyes crossed and walk toward us with stiff arms and

Me in a ballet skirt outside
the Big House, 1949

Penny Jencks outside one of my father's
army barracks houses overlooking the
beach, Cape Cod, c. 1955

legs as if she were a zombie. Blair and I fled, but we laughed so hard I had to hold my crotch in order not to pee. Penny told ghost stories. "The Green Man" was the scariest. In a low voice, she would say, "I'm on the first step, I'm on the second step, the third step . . ." The higher up the stairs she got the more scared we became. The story ended with, "Gotcha!" She also taught us a song about a witch: "There was an old woman all skin and bone, woo, woo, woo, woo," etc. Penny sometimes turned up at our house on her horse Bobby. She let us climb on his back. Bobby loved Penny and she loved him more than anything else, I think.

Later that summer our father returned from France and took Blair and me to Lobster Lake in northern Maine. His mother, whom we called Gaga, had inherited a fishing camp from one of her brothers who had been gassed in World War I and died young. She and my grandfather had spent many vacations there accompanied by their four children and a group of servants who they put up in a large tent. To get to the Lobster Lake camp, we drove to Greenville on the southern end of Moosehead Lake, bought supplies, and then drove on to North East Carry at the lake's north shore. There

Blair and me on the way to Lobster Lake, 1949

we met up with Jack Hall and his second wife, Jean. (His first wife, Dodie, had run off with a Provincetown fisherman.) We packed our things in two long canoes, to which the men attached small outboard motors, and we started down Lobster Stream.

Part of the river was clogged with logs upon which stood lumberjacks prodding the logs with poles that had hooks and spikes at their ends. I watched to see if a log would roll and a lumberjack would fall in the water. They never did. It took quite a while to get through the log jam, and this annoyed our father who had a huge boil covered with a gauze bandage on his left hand. He didn't complain, but I knew it hurt because he was even quieter than usual. Blair and I scanned the shore for moose. Way ahead we would see something large and dark and sometimes it wasn't a boulder. Sometimes it was a moose with its nose in the water eating vegetation near the river's edge. When we got close the moose would rise out of the river dripping, and, with its strange, ungainly gait, vanish into the brush.

After an hour or so, Lobster Stream opened out on to Lobster Lake. We crossed the lake, entered a small cove, pulled up the canoes, and hauled our knapsacks and food supplies uphill to the camp, which comprised several log cabins. The two biggest, one for eating and the other for sleeping, were connected by a wooden walkway. Above the entrance door of the kitchen-dining room cabin was the head of a stag. To the left and right of the mammoth stone fireplace in the sleeping cabin hung dark brown bearskins. It took a while to get used to all these dead animals, testimony to hunting and killing and violence. The adults slept in the two ground floor bedrooms, and Blair and I climbed a ladder to a loft equipped with camp beds. Here, under the eaves, were relics from the past—a wind-up Victrola that actually worked. The adults put away the groceries. There wasn't much. Our father was indifferent to food. Also, he had an ethic that if you were camping, you

My father on the walkway between log cabins,
Lobster Lake, 1949

were supposed to travel light and make do with the most basic provisions. Mostly we ate canned ham or peanut butter and jelly sandwiches. Blair and I got really sick of canned ham. It was cold and the jelly around it was disgusting.

It didn't take long for tensions to arise between Jack and Jean Hall. I don't think my father liked Jean. She was tough and always red in the face from alcohol. Jack was a drinker, too. During his temper tantrums his face became dark and scary. Jean just shrieked. She hated our camp. It was too isolated and there was no electricity, no plumbing, and no telephone. There were two outhouses, and at night, because there might be a bear, she was afraid of walking the short way downhill to get to one of them. Jean Hall became so crazy that Jack had to take her home to Wellfleet. Good! Now Blair and I had our father all to ourselves. Also, with the Halls gone, he didn't drink so much whiskey, and during the day he took us on canoe trips to picnic beaches all over the lake. My favorite was called Hayden's Rock where, beneath an enormous boulder, big enough to climb on if you were brave, lay a beach of shiny, smooth black pebbles that got hot in the sun. I liked to think that this rock was named after me. Later I learned that it was named after Gaga's mother, Annie Hayden Hyde.

One excursion that took us away from the lake was to a logging camp deep in the woods. The ground there was thick mud and there were pigs rutting about in it. Off to one side were several log cabins and some menacing logging machines. A few large unshaven men watched us from their cabin steps. My father strolled up to them. Blair and I kept our distance. In his best Brahmin accent, he asked them how they were doing. They grunted in reply. Our father asked if it was possible to buy some pork. They said they didn't have any. It was clear to me that they just wanted us to go away. I was sure they had guns, and they looked at Blair and me as if they were sizing us up like trees they planned to fell. When we were finally on our way back to our camp, I told my father that I thought they were bad men. Oh no, he said. They're just lonely and being lonely makes men angry.

Our father was lonely, but we did not know it. One morning he announced that he was taking the canoe and going to the little grocery store at North East Carry to buy a box of Hershey bars. It was amazing—he would make that two-hour trip just in order to buy something that Blair and I liked. Years later he told me he had gone to North East Carry to see if there was a letter from Mougouch who had remained in Europe and was probably enjoying a tryst with Matta. My father returned from North East Carry with the promised chocolate bars and a bottle of milk, but without a letter. He looked sad. That night I stayed awake for a long time listening to the loons calling to one another.

17

The Manheims

Photographs show that at some point late in the summer of 1949, Blair and I lived with our mother in a rickety house on a rickety wharf in the west end of Provincetown—I think it was called Captain Jack's Wharf. Here, if the tide was high, I could hear breaking waves beneath the old floorboards. Stan Thayer was in and out of our house all the time. He must have been my mother's lover.

Early in September, our mother took us to the New York Store opposite the MacMillan Wharf in the center of Provincetown. She bought us winter clothes, and she bought us each a peashooter,

Blair and me on the end of Captain
Jack's Wharf, Provincetown, 1949

which is a wider and firmer version of a drinking straw and into which you insert a dried pea and then blow it out into the world. We moved back into the Big House, and a short time later she told us that she was going to Mexico again and that a nice couple, Ralph and Mary Manheim, were going to live with us in the Big House. The Manheims had two daughters: Kate, who was four, and Nora, who was about two. It would be lots of fun. We would go to an excellent public school in Truro. Ralph had a soft voice, and he always looked concerned as if he was worrying about the state of the world. My mother told us that he was a well-known translator who had lived in Germany and had translated Hitler's *Mein Kampf*. Ralph talked about serious topics like politics, which my parents ignored. Mary, of Irish Catholic descent, looked anxious and worn and much older than Ralph. She made an effort to be cheerful and most of the time she was loving.

After my mother drove away, promising to be back next summer, I lay on my back under a huge pine tree below the front steps of the Big House. The pine-needle-covered earth was like a mat-

Ralph and Mary Manheim,
Cape Cod, 1949

Kate and Nora Manheim, 1949

tress. I wanted my mind to be just as soft, but the inside of my skull felt chunky and hard, full of sharp corners. Everything awful was in there, and it kept tumbling around. I did that crunch down thing on my heart, and instead of missing my mother, I studied the patches of blue sky in the spaces between the pine tree's branches. High up there were pine cones, black against the sky. If they moved, I knew they were birds. When the wind picked up, the blue pieces of sky changed shape. Embraced by the pine's limbs, these blue shapes seemed both close and far, so near that I could have climbed the tree and put my arm through them, and so far away that they were part of an emptiness that went on forever. Now that I was eight, I no longer pictured a brick dome enclosing our sky and blocking out infinity. The vastness going on and on and the whirring sound of the wind in the pine's branches made me feel alone. I went indoors where familiar objects—the ivory crocodile, my father's desk lamp—offered comfort. And Blair was there.

Every morning Ralph drove Blair and me out to Route 6 where we waited for the Truro public school's principal to pick us up and drive us to school, a long, white clapboard building in North Truro. As usual when Blair and I entered a new school, fall term had already begun. When the teacher walked me back to my desk at least twenty heads turned and looked at me. I hated to be looked at. If someone looked closely, they would see so many defects, especially my tummy even though I tried to hold it in. Luckily there was one girl I already knew from last summer in Provincetown, Gaby Rilleau, the daughter of Roger Rilleau who made Greek-type sandals in a shop in Provincetown's East End.

At the beginning of the school day, the teacher asked the class to stand and say the Lord's Prayer followed by the Pledge of Allegiance to the flag of the United States of America. Both were new to me, so I just moved my lips. We were supposed to stand on the left side of our desks and salute the flag with our right hand placed across our breast. On the first day I saluted with my left hand and stood on the wrong side of my desk. I was mortified, but no one seemed to notice because just as we finished the pledge, there was a commotion. A boy was bent over his desk with a pool of vomit at his feet. This boy vomited almost every morning, I was told. He must be so ashamed. Someone brought a pail of sand and poured it over the mess and the whole class filed out of the classroom while the vomit was cleaned up.

At recess, I went out and sat under a pitch pine. Gaby Rilleau joined me. From that day on, at every recess, we sat together under this tree. I didn't want to know anyone else. The rest of the people in my class were not gentle like Gaby. I don't think they liked the idea of a person who had lived somewhere other than Cape Cod. Even though I had come to Cape Cod straight from the Boston hospital where I was born, I was considered to be a "wash-ashore." I taught Gaby how to make pine needle chains—another thing that George Senseney had taught me. Recess was long enough for us to each make a necklace or a crown. Blair had recess at a different time from me. She told me that during recess boys threw pebbles at her ankles. It didn't hurt, but it made her know how much the boys disliked her. To them, she was a foreigner.

Teaching at the Truro Public School was rigidly programmed, and I was far behind my classmates in arithmetic and grammar. At Dalton and Hickory Ridge I had always printed my letters, but at this Truro school I learned to write cursive script according to the Palmer Method. Making loop after loop run across paper was a pleasure. I had to work hard. Public school was different from Dalton and Hickory Ridge. At those "progressive" schools, there were no marks, and no competition. Here our work sheets came back with our mark written in red pencil at the top.

After school the principal drove Blair and me to the end of our dirt road and we walked the mile and a half to the Big House. The first part of the walk was fun because we passed what we called Turtle Pond (now named Black Pond). We always approached it on tiptoe in order not to disturb the turtles. I didn't dare step into the pond's muck, but if a turtle was about two feet offshore I could grab him, take him home to Horseleech Pond, and set him free. There were turtles in Horseleech, too, but not as many. And there were huge snapping turtles with heads bigger than a grownup's fist and strong mouths that could snap your arm off or drag you down to the pond's bottom.

The walk home from school took us past Anna and Norman Matson's driveway, then came Herring Pond on the right, then Slough Pond on the left. Here we might stop to swim. About six feet out from shore under about three feet of water was a cement box half buried in sand. Someone had told Blair that there was a dead man buried inside, so we kept our distance. A little farther along the road, if you looked carefully you could see the sluice-way between Williams and Gull Ponds. Next came the Chermayeffs' driveway and finally we arrived at our own driveway with Horseleech Pond on the left.

The only bad part of this whole walk was going up a long hill and past a black house said to be a hunter's cabin. No one lived there. Even the windows looked black. I was convinced that murderers lurked inside waiting to rush out and attack whoever passed. Long-legged Blair was always far ahead of me. Trying to sound really plaintive, I would cry my usual "Wait for me!" Blair did not listen. Once I screamed for her to stop because, just before the murderer's house, a long black snake lay curled on the sandy road. She did not come back to see the snake, and it slithered into the bushes. I had no problem with garter snakes. Indeed, one summer I took my pet garter snake with me when I spent the night at a friend's house. In the middle of the night I woke up with my snake wound around my neck. I put it back in its can and the next morning it was dead.

In November and December, it was almost dark when Blair and I reached home. I was so happy to see the lights on in the Big House and even happier when I went inside, and Mary Manheim was at the stove dropping doughnut batter into a huge vat of boiling oil. She gave us doughnuts to warm our hands. To me Mary Manheim seemed the nicest woman in the world. But, remembering her sometimes desperate face, I think she made doughnuts to stifle her rage.

Things got bad when Mary found out that Ralph was having an affair with Anna Matson. Ralph and Anna were both good-looking, highly sensual, and passionate about issues of social welfare. For Anna, living such an isolated life in the Wellfleet woods and married to a man much too old for her, being with Ralph must have been liberating. Norman could be tyrannical. He had a weak heart and, according to my mother, he warned Anna that he would have a heart attack if she left him. One time when he found out that she was being unfaithful, Norman took his revenge by taking their two children away and having them baptized as Catholics. Anna had no idea where Little Anna and Peter had gone.

Mary Manheim was increasingly miserable. I do not remember Ralph being around much. It was just Mary, Blair, and me, and Kate and Nora. The doughnut making became more frenetic. Mary looked as if she wanted to hit somebody with the tongs with which she pulled the doughnuts from the bubbling oil. As winter closed in and it was too cold to play outside, Blair and I sat on the living room floor and played dominos, Parcheesi, checkers, and card games such as War or Go Fish. These days when Mary came through the living room to get to her bedroom a tension filled the air like a hum. I could almost feel it with my fingertips. One day when Blair and I were playing Parcheesi, Nora and Kate grabbed some of our Parcheesi pieces and ran off with them. Blair and I were furious—this was our house and our Parcheesi set: Kate and Nora had no right to take our things. Mary came in and screamed at us as she swept our dominos off our father's desk and onto the floor.

Ralph must have written to our parents to tell them that the situation had become untenable. We couldn't live with the Manheims anymore. What to do with Blair and me was a problem. During the next months my father and my mother fought over where Blair and I should live. He started a custody case at the Barnstable Court on the grounds that our mother had deserted her children. He wanted us to come and live with him and Mougouch in France. Our mother refused to let us go. She decided that Blair and I should join her in Mexico, and she kept writing us letters telling us what a marvelous time we would have if we lived with her. Blair and I had, Ralph Manheim told our father, "been sold and unsold on Mexico two or three times." Our father thought that our mother's Mexico propaganda was immoral.

After a while our mother said she would come to Cape Cod and live with us in the Big House. But she didn't come. She stayed in Mexico because it turned out that she wasn't needed: our grandmother had offered to have us live with her. For a while our father kept trying to get custody, but in the end, he was too busy with Mougouch and her daughters and his Marshall Plan job to continue fighting. He wrote to his mother: "The only way I could get custody now would be to drop everything and come right back to U.S." And he wasn't willing to do that.

18

Gaga

That Christmas we had two Christmases, one with the Man-heims and one with Gaga, who lived alone in a big house at 63 Garden Street in Cambridge, Massachusetts. When Ralph explained that we were going to live with our grandmother I was glad. Cape Cod in December is dismal—windy, bleak, and dark by three-thirty in the afternoon. The summer people's houses are closed up. It is lonely. Anyway, I loved Gaga. She was my happy, well-heeled grand-mother, not desperate like my mother's mother. She had elegant clothes, broad-brimmed hats, real pearls, and she always smelled like expensive talcum powder. She lived in a three-story house on the corner of Garden and Linnaean Streets. It had a huge garden enclosed by a solid wooden fence, a safe place for Echo, Gaga's big beautifully groomed brown poodle, to run around in. We were to live with Gaga until summer, so she enrolled us in the Buckingham School where we started on January 3, 1950. Every day, as we set out across Garden Street on our walk to school, Gaga would wave to us from a second-floor window. Her waves felt like hugs.

Mary Manheim's doughnuts had made Blair and me fat—or fat-ter. Gaga called us her two pet elephants. She made our big stom-achs seem adorable. At meals, we would slide down the banister and race each other in order to be the first to stand behind our grandmother's dining room chair. Gaga liked to have us pull out her chair and then push it back in as she sat down. We believed that if we did this, she would love us even more.

Gaga had two servants who lived on the third floor, a cook named Bessie and a maid named Annie. They were both elderly Irish women with white hair and pale fat arms. The food cooked by Bessie and served by Annie was the best I had ever eaten. For dessert Bessie made Floating Island, which was a molded pudding made of egg whites over which we poured a light-yellow custard sauce. Between courses Gaga rang a little bell. Annie would come in and clear the table. Gaga asked Blair and me to help by taking our plates into the kitchen. She told us to compliment Bessie on the delicious meal. Gaga taught us manners. Our mother never bothered about things such as how you place your fork and knife on your plate when you have finished eating. At Gaga's house we even had finger bowls.

Gaga's placemats were made of some kind of board and each one had an image of a different kind of duck surrounded by a gray-green border. In the middle of Gaga's mahogany table lay a mirror upon which swam two Chinese porcelain Mandarin ducks, a colorful male and his duller brown wife. One day when I was lifting the male duck's

Blair and me, 1949, in Gaga's music room. Behind Blair, a lion skin rug from a lion supposedly shot by our father

Gaga (our paternal grandmother, Eleanor Hayden Hyde Phillips)

lid to look inside, I broke off the tip of his wing. This was the end of the world, I thought, but Gaga didn't punish me. I knew that she loved these ducks very much, especially because her late husband had been a duck expert. Gaga's not showing her sadness was kind. Maybe she had brought those ducks back from China when she went there as a young woman and met the Empress. She had many Chinese and Japanese objects, which she kept in a cabinet with a glass door and a light inside. Gaga would take lacquer medicine boxes out of the cabinet and show us how they opened into several compartments and she let us handle her collection of carved ivory netsuke. The figures of wise men squatting or children playing set off stories in my mind.

Some of these objects had been bought by my grandfather John Charles Phillips, who traveled all over the world acquiring artifacts for Harvard's Peabody Museum as well as bird and animal specimens (horns, antlers, and heads of mammals) for the Louis Agassiz Museum of Comparative Zoology. He had trained to be a doctor but, after graduating from Harvard Medical School in 1904 and a two-year stint at the Boston City Hospital, he decided he did not want to practice medicine. The only time he did practice was when he was in charge of a field hospital during World War I.

What he did do was write books and articles about wildlife conservation, hunting, ducks, animal breeding, and genetics. (Like many well-heeled Bostonians, he wanted to keep races pure and wrote articles about Eugenics.) My grandfather also traveled. In1896 he accompanied Robert Edwin Peary as far as Greenland on a North Pole expedition. In 1906 he traveled from Japan to Korea and then on to hunt tigers in the south of China. Later he traveled all over America spending part of one winter hunting mountain lions and peccaries in the Arizona mountains. There were several trips to Egypt where, legend has it, in March 1908 my father was conceived at (actually on) the Temple of Luxor. Two years before I was born, while grouse hunting in New Hampshire, my grandfather died of a heart attack just as his dog came to a point, the bird flew, and he raised his gun.

While my grandfather traveled, Gaga mostly stayed home and looked after their two sons and two daughters. Sometimes she accompanied her husband, for example, on an African safari in 1923. She and her three younger children had been living in Paris for a year while my fourteen-year-old father attended Le Rosey, a fancy boarding school in Switzerland. When he had completed the second volume of *A Natural History of the Ducks*, my grandfather joined his family for two months in the south of France after which he took Gaga and my father on a safari in Kenya. On this trip he collected fish, birds, small rodents, and occasionally, my father recalled, heads and horns. My father loved telling me about saving Gaga's life when a lion came after her and she climbed a thorn tree and he shot the lion. To prove it, he pointed to the lion skin carpet on Gaga's music room floor.

When her husband was gone for months and months, Gaga became depressed. I think they then called it "having the vapors." In spite of her active social life, living with young children on Mount Vernon Street on Boston's Beacon Hill, or, during the summer months, in a grand house overlooking Wenham Lake west of Boston, must have been lonely. And not being able to fulfill her wish to be an opera singer was painful, especially when her cousin Emma Eames (who, like Gaga was brought up in Bath, Maine) had a career as a major diva, singing to great acclaim at venues such as the Paris Opera, London's Covent Garden, and New York City's Metropolitan Opera. In my grandfather's circle, it was considered inappropriate for a Boston lady to go on a public stage, so Gaga took part in opera performances at the Vincent Club, a women's organization. For a while Gaga was so unhappy she had to stay at Dr. Riggs's sanatorium in Stockbridge, Massachusetts.

In Gaga's music room there was a trunk full of the costumes that she had worn for her opera performances. The most exotic was her costume for *Aida*. With the help of a few safety pins, it fit Blair, but it was way too big for me. Gaga had two grand pianos. She would play, and Blair and I would dress up in costumes and dance. Or we would stand behind the piano and sing songs that Gaga taught us. My favorite was "The April Girl," the lyrics of which describe the advantages enjoyed by girls born in March, April, and May. The best were April girls. Being born in May, as Blair was, was pretty good, too, but there was nothing special about November girls like me. When we sang, Blair stood closest to Gaga so she could read the notes and words on the score. I couldn't see that far, so I never really learned to sing. When she grew up, Blair became a singer. I learned to play the piano instead. Probably Gaga was just trying to encourage the ugly duckling when she told me that I was more musical than Blair, but I wanted to believe it. I knew enough not to repeat what she had said, but I kept it in my head, something to hold on to, something that gave me a secret strength.

Around New Year's, Aunt Madelyn, the elder of my father's two younger sisters, came to visit. She had recently played the lead in *South Pacific*, probably not on Broadway, and during her visit she sat on the floor next to the Christmas tree and sang "I'm gonna wash that man right out of my hair" while pretending to rub shampoo into her scalp. Such a glamorous woman! Before she came, I had known my aunt only from a large Lydia Field Emmet portrait of Madelyn and her younger sister, Nina. Dressed in filmy pale pink dresses, the girls looked so well cared for. It was as though they lived in a secret garden, a garden with no worries.

On another wall in Gaga's house hung Emmet's portrait of my father at about age six. With his brown shorts and jacket and long hair, he reminded me of Little Lord Fauntleroy. He looked wistful. As a child, he was sick a lot, and he told me that Gaga made him drink barley water. Gaga still had funny ideas about medicine. If Blair or I were grumpy, she assumed that we were constipated and insisted that we swallow a tablespoon of Phillips' Milk of Magnesia, which tasted like chalk. My father was his mother's favorite, perhaps because he was sickly or because he was her firstborn. Maybe her attachment to him was part of the reason he stuttered until he was in his twenties. Even though he was groomed to be a diplomat like his uncle William Phillips, who served twice as under secretary of state as well as ambassador to Belgium and later to Italy, my father became an artist. That way he did not have to talk.

Gaga was religious. I knew nothing about religion except the Lord's Prayer that we had recited at the Truro school. On Gaga's bedside table was a booklet called *The Daily Word*. I opened it up and saw that it had a holy idea for each day. I didn't open it again. It looked boring. Going with Gaga to the Episcopal Trinity Church in Boston on Sundays was fun, partly because we got to dress up and Gaga was so proud of us when, after the service, she introduced us to members of the congregation. After church she sometimes took us to the Chilton Club, where we met some of her women friends. Before we went to bed Gaga taught us to say our prayers. I kneeled next to my bed and said, "Now I lay me down to sleep. I pray the Lord my soul to keep. If I should die before I wake, I pray the Lord my soul to take." Aunt Madelyn later taught me a version that had no death in it: "Now I lay me down to sleep, Father in heaven watch over me. I pray my sleep be sound and sweet, and my waking happy be."

We said Gaga's version every night, but after a few weeks, since I hadn't died yet, the death part lost its menace. With Gaga on her knees beside me, wearing a nightgown and a quilted pink silk bathrobe, I felt protected. Her face was shiny from Helena Rubinstein lanolin cream. I used to watch her sit at her dressing table, her hair covered with a cotton cap, as she squeezed an inch of the heavy pungent cream out of the tube and smoothed it over the thin loose skin of her cheeks and forehead. Once she had tucked us into bed, Gaga sang lullabies. She knew the usual ones such as "To and fro, so soft and slow . . ." That one was best for falling asleep, but she knew much more interesting lullabies. I always wanted her to sing, "Would you know the baby's skies? Baby's skies are Mama's eyes. Mama's eyes and smile together make the baby's pleasant weather."

Even though Gaga loved us and enjoyed having Blair and me live with her, she also liked to feel martyred. She sighed a lot. We were a big responsibility. Often, she said she was tired. Gaga also liked to blame and criticize. She especially enjoyed finding fault with our mother. Lybie was, Gaga said, irresponsible, selfish, unreliable, and overly concerned with her own beauty. Gaga almost never got angry. She just got grumpy. But once she got angry with Blair, because Blair and Aunt Nina's oldest daughter, Nancy Washburn, found a snake in the garden and brought it up to the bathroom so that it could swim in the tub. When the snake vanished down the drain and reemerged in Gaga's bathtub, Gaga was not amused. Another time Gaga got angry at me—I do not remember what for—and she spanked me with a hairbrush. I was outraged. I had never been spanked before. I went to my room and refused to come out. Blair played peacekeeper. She told Gaga that she should not have done that. Gaga felt sorry and I stopped being mad.

During the first weeks in Cambridge, Blair and I shared a room, but then Gaga decided that, because of the three-and-a-half years' difference in age, we each ought to have our own room. My bedroom was large, larger than any bedroom I had ever had, but I liked Blair's sunny corner room better. At the foot of her bed was a chaise longue with a salmon-pink flower print slipcover. Her bedspread was pink, too. My room was blue, a subtle grayish blue that made the room seem cold. Each of our rooms had two four-poster beds. The dark wooden bedposts were topped by carvings that looked like elongated acorns. I could hold onto two posts and swing between the beds. Gaga did not approve of this. She was afraid that her overweight grandchild would break the bedposts.

Without Blair in the bed next to mine, I was afraid of the dark, and Gaga's room was way down the hall. After Gaga finished saying good night and closed my door, I tried to hold on to the comfort of her smell and song. I pushed away thoughts of danger. What helped was counting the beams of light that went around the walls of my room when cars passed on Garden Street. Counting how many beams came from the right and how many from the left lulled me into sleep.

A shared bathroom connected Blair's and my bedrooms. Instead of a roll of toilet paper, it had a metal box on the wall next to the toilet. Gaga showed us how to pull sheets of toilet paper out of it—not too many. She didn't want to waste paper. The paper was stiff, like newsprint, but I got used to it. Next to the toilet was a huge old-fashioned tub. The water gushed out of the faucet fast, and, as the tub filled, the bathwater turned a very pale green and smelled of minerals. Sometimes I filled the tub up to my neck. I was not supposed to do this because Gaga wanted to save water.

Hanging on the bathroom wall, between two windows was a black-and-white print by my father. It was semi-abstract with two shapes that I could recognize—a checkerboard and a piece of crinkled paper going up in flames. It must have been a student work from the early 1930s when my father studied in Paris with Fernand Léger. Like Léger's work at that time, the print mixed Cubism and Surrealism. To me, the burning paper was haunting. What did it mean? Why did he do it? My mother had been in Léger's class at the same time as my father. Two 1932 photographs of her sitting close to Léger and certainly the most beautiful woman in the room, suggest that she was his prize pupil. A year later, Léger even wrote a highly complimentary text for the brochure of her first exhibition in New York. My father was not interested in my mother back then. She was too skinny and too melancholy, he said.

Gaga made us take naps. We didn't have to sleep, just rest. In Blair's room there was a shelf piled high with old *National Geo-*

graphic magazines. I picked up a copy because Blair was reading one and even though the print looked small, I thought I had better try. I carried a stack of them to my room and climbed onto my bed. Soon I realized that I didn't have to read the text. I could just look at the pictures and read the captions. Until I saw these magazines, I had had no idea that there were so many different ways to live on this planet. At first the photographs of African women naked to the waist shocked me. Many of the women had long narrow breasts that hung straight down like a cow's udder. I hoped that when I got older, I would have high round breasts like my mother's.

Another thing I did during naps was to draw birds. Gaga had shown us the four volumes of our grandfather's *A Natural History of the Ducks*. With reverence, she gently pulled back the translucent onionskin papers that protected each illustration. We were not allowed to take these heavy books to our rooms. Instead Gaga gave me a young person's bird book and encouraged me to copy and learn the names of all the different birds. On the walls of our bedrooms hung Audubon prints—much too complicated for me to

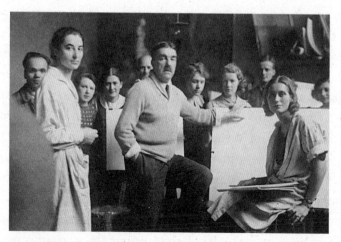

Viera da Silva (standing left), Fernand Léger (center),
and my mother (seated right), 1932

copy. The birds in the Audubon prints looked so alive I almost thought I should tiptoe in order not to disturb them.

Afternoon tea was a formal event for Gaga. She sat in the middle of the sofa with the tea tray set on the low table right in front of her. She wore one of two tea gowns, one red, one blue, both full-length and made of soft silk velvet. After letting the Hu-Kwa tea steep, she would pour us each a cup to which she added milk and a lump of sugar. The best thing on the tea tray was the cupcakes with vanilla frosting that Bessie made fresh every day. Almost as good was the thinly sliced white bread spread with butter. At teatime the slices of bread were laid out on a plate in an overlapping row. You picked one up and folded it into four and put it on your small plate. Sinking my teeth into the buttered layers was an immense pleasure. Hoping no one would notice how greedy I was, I took at least three slices.

Bessie showed me how she sliced the bread on a circular blade attached to a kitchen counter—a dangerous-looking machine that we were warned never to touch. Sometimes I went with Bessie to buy this bread at the bakery a few blocks away on Linnaean Street. She would also buy a newspaper and give me the page with the funnies. On weekends we were allowed to visit Bessie and Annie on the third floor. Their bedrooms had low, slanted ceilings and their beds had iron headboards painted white. Annie taught us how to knit. The hardest part was putting the first row of wool onto the knitting needle. I loved the *click* and then the sliding noise when I put a needle into an existing stich. As my ball of wool became a scarf, I marveled: I had actually made something!

After tea Gaga read to us. Her favorites were Kipling's *Jungle Book*s and what she called the "Lobster Books," which had stories about lobsters living at the bottom of the sea. Sometimes Gaga had guests for tea, mostly men. Like my father, Gaga was a brilliant flirt. She was brought up that it was good manners to make other people feel they were delightful. Her intelligence, wit, and her charming dimple drew people to her. A frequent guest was the poet Archibald MacLeish, who had just started teaching at Harvard. He was so distinguished looking that I didn't dare open my mouth. In any case, in those days everyone told us that "Children are to be seen and not heard." So, it was okay to be shy. Another formidable Harvard professor who came to tea was the lawyer Archibald Cox, who twenty-three years later was appointed special prosecutor during the Watergate scandal and whose firing by President Nixon became known as the Saturday Night Massacre. Arthur Schlesinger, then an associate professor of history at Harvard, came at least once, and there was a man named Mark De Wolfe Howe, a Harvard Law School professor who was Gaga's close, close friend.

Mr. Howe had three daughters. The younger two, Susan and Fanny, were Blair's and my ages and they became our Cambridge best friends. Fanny had straight blond hair and a roundish face—*gamin* might be the word to describe her. She was smart and funny, full of mischief, and game for anything. When her parents rented a house on the bay side in Truro, I spent nights there. (That's where my garter snake died.) At low tide Fanny and I would walk out in the salt marsh below her house and look for shells among the reeds. Normally I was afraid of mud,

Fanny Howe, me, and Mary Barton Potter,
Cape Cod, 1950

especially the smelly mud under the reeds on the bayside. I had seen crabs come out of holes and worse still, long sea worms. With Fanny everything seemed safe. Her older sister Susan was beautiful, but more severe than Fanny. She had a temper. Susan is the only person with whom I have ever had a physical fight. I can't remember what it was about, but we rolled on the ground and tore at each other's hair. When they grew up, both Fanny and Susan became poets.

Soon after we arrived at 63 Garden Street, Gaga expressed her shock at our shabby ill-fitting clothes. Part of her disapproval was prompted by her disapproval of our mother's neglectful ways. She took us to Filene's department store in downtown Boston. In the children's department, she found a section where they sold a line of clothing for fat children called Chubbettes, and there she outfitted Blair and me with clothes that would get us through from winter to summer. Gaga seemed pleased with her purchases, which was a relief, because she wasn't one who liked to spend money. On our Boston outings, Gaga would treat Blair and me to a ride on one of the Swan Boats in the Public Garden. The boats were paddled around the pond by a man concealed in a paddle box that was hidden inside a huge white swan. Gaga also liked to feed the ducks, tossing them crusts of bread. I guessed that she liked ducks so much because of her husband's fascination with them.

Gaga wanted Blair and me to know about Boston and about our Bostonian background. She wanted us to know about her heritage, too. Gaga was from Bath, Maine. Her maiden name was Eleanor Hayden Hyde. Her father, Thomas Hyde, was, according to Gaga, the youngest brigadier general on the Union side in the Civil War. In the midst of a battle he had heard a southern officer shout, "Shoot that little general on the white horse!" When the war was over, Thomas Hyde started the Bath Iron Works, which made boats, especially ships for the navy. Now the Bath Iron Works extends over a huge stretch of Bath's shoreline, and much of what it is building is a military secret.

Recognizing her daughter Eleanor's lively intelligence, Gaga's parents let her apply to Radcliffe College. Gaga loved to tell us the story of her admissions interview. She wore a fashionable wide-brimmed, feather-decked hat that she had just acquired in Paris. The hat was a mistake. The admissions people thought Gaga was frivolous, so they admitted her only as a "special" student. Nevertheless, she loved her years of study. Every day she did her homework—mostly short essays—while traveling from Boston to Cambridge on the streetcar.

Because Gaga was from Maine, she felt that she had married someone from a higher social stratum than her own. She told us that our grandfather was from one of the great Boston families. We learned that our ancestor George Phillips graduated with two degrees from Gonville & Caius College, Cambridge University, in 1617, served as vicar of Boxted in Essex, and came to America in 1630 aboard the *Arbella*, the flagship of the Winthrop fleet whose eleven boats carried seven hundred Puritans from England to the Massachusetts Bay Colony. During the crossing, Phillips's sermons boosted morale, and Governor John Winthrop praised him, saying, "We have much cause to bless God for him." Phillips probably wrote and was one of the seven signers of Winthop's *Humble Request*, a polite but subtly sarcastic parting missive to the King and Church of England. Upon arrival in Salem, George Phillips and Richard Saltonstall traveled up the Charles River and founded Watertown for which Phillips wrote the Covenant signed by forty-one men. That same year, 1630, Phillips founded the First Congregational Church in Watertown, Massachusetts, where he served as minister until his death in 1644.

The next two important ancestors were Samuel Phillips, who founded Phillips Academy Andover in 1778, and his uncle, John Phillips, who founded Phillips Exeter Academy in 1781. Samuel Phillips's great-grandson was Phillips Brooks, a brilliant preacher who was rector of Trinity Church and who oversaw the church's rebuilding after the Great Boston Fire of 1872. He also wrote the lyrics for the Christmas carol "O Little Town of Bethlehem." Another ancestor named John Phillips served as the first mayor of Boston in 1822. His son, Wendell Phillips, was an abolitionist famous for his powerful oratory. Wendell Phillips joined the anti-slavery movement after witnessing the (failed) lynching of abolitionist William Lloyd Garrison, with whom he became a close associate. He also fought for the rights of women and Native Americans. Wendell Phillips was the ancestor of whom Gaga was most proud. She took Blair and me to see his statue in the Boston Public Garden and she told us that, because of his speeches against slavery, he was stoned in the streets of Boston. In his statue he is holding a broken chain. I was amazed to have come from such people. I hoped that I might have inherited some of their courage. Living with Gaga, I began to feel like a Bostonian. It was, after all, the city of my birth.

In May, Gaga gave Blair and me boxes of pansies and trowels with which to plant them beside her garden's fence. The idea of putting something into the earth and having it take root gave me a feeling of everything being ongoing. Luckily, I did not know that pansies are annuals.

Portrait of John Phillips, founder of
Phillips Exeter Academy

19

Naked

In June 1950, while he was still in France, my father let my mother use the Turkey Houses. She acted as though she still owned the place, holding up one of Dasya's flowered plates, remarking on how vulgar it was, and then pushing a stack of Dasya's dishes behind a stack of her own Mexican earthenware bowls. She took the old bureaus and bedside tables out of the cabins, stood them on the pine needle–covered path, and painted them in different interesting colors—yellow-ochre, rust red, gray-blue. She even took a knife and paired down the edges of the bureau drawers to make them slide in and out. That was the part of my mother that I loved. She could fix up the world.

During those weeks, my father sent Blair and me photographs he had taken of Maro and Natasha and Mougouch who was five months' pregnant, but you couldn't tell. To celebrate our future sibling's birth, Blair and I took our knitting needles and balls of pale yellow wool up to the bearberry-covered knoll on the back side of the high dune below which lay our beach. There we sat— knit, purl, knit, purl—as we struggled to follow knitting instructions for baby's booties and a sweater. When we became tired of knitting, we practiced backbends, handstands, cartwheels, and flips. If we fell, the bearberry was soft and springy. Flips and cartwheels were among the few things that I could do better than Blair.

Blair and I often rowed across Horseleech Pond and climbed the hill at the far end. Back then the hill was covered with bearberry.

Mougouch, pregnant with my sister
Antonia, Orgeval, France, 1950

There were almost no trees, and from the summit you could see all the ponds. Once we took sleeping bags, flashlights, and peanut butter sandwiches and spent the night there. Blair did not always agree with me about the choice of camping spot. She preferred a place partway up the hill sheltered by four or five pine trees. I wanted to be on top of the hill, out in the open. Blair usually had her way because she would say, "Fine, you can sleep wherever you want, but I am going to sleep under the pines."

This was the summer when I learned to be modest. It happened in an instant. I walked over the hill to Dwight Macdonald's house—one of the three army barracks houses that my father had constructed on Slough Pond. Dwight's son Mike was there with his two friends, Charlie Jencks (Penny's younger brother) and Reuel Wilson (Edmund Wilson and Mary McCarthy's son). The boys were in the water and I was about to take off my clothes and plunge in when I noticed that they all had on bathing suits. They were a year or two older than me. Something had changed. Maybe if I had been thin, I wouldn't have minded them seeing me naked, but my nine-year-old body felt like something that eyes might notice and appraise. Feeling sad because I liked the feel of Slough Pond's water, I sat on the shore and watched the boys. Horseleech Pond's water is velvety, perhaps because so much vegetation grows in it. Slough Pond has fewer lily pads and less animal life. I always imagine it to be full of minerals that keep its water transparent and clean.

This was probably the summer in which I began to dislike my mother's body. I did not know it by touch. My mother was not someone who hugged or even put her arms around another person. I knew her body by sight, and sometimes it was embarrassing. Her bosoms were especially irritating. She always left too many of the buttons on her shirt undone and she didn't wear a bra. She didn't even bother to put a towel around her when she walked from her turkey cabin to the pond.

At one of her lunchtime beach picnics my mother and a few of her friends gathered right at the bottom of the dune. When Penny Jencks, Blair, and I took the path from the Turkey Houses to our ocean beach and came over the dune and saw all the naked grown-ups, we sat on the outskirts of their circle. Mary Grand, a woman of more than Rubenesque proportions, seemed not in the least chagrinned by the rolls of fat below her belly button. Beside her sat Dwight Macdonald sprawled with his legs straight out. His penis and testicles were so pale and ugly that I had to look away. In spite of his unabashed nakedness, Dwight remained my favorite adult. He understood what children wanted. Once a week he would take a bunch of us to the movies in Wellfleet, and he always asked the ticket lady to give us movie posters. Mine was of Montgomery Clift, the actor I most adored.

I should have been used to naked grown-ups. Nudity was the tradition on what was then called Phillips Beach. Once when my mother and a group of her friends were sunbathing naked on our beach, a fat man who they knew to be a voyeur came along and stopped and goggled. My mother jumped up and ran at him hoping to chase him away. Terrified of her naked body, the man turned and rushed along the shore as fast as he could go. Not only did my mother and father swim naked, I was told that in the 1930s they sometimes walked to cocktails at other people's houses in the nude. My mother was not ashamed. She knew her body was beautiful.

My mother's idea of a picnic was sloppy. She never prepared sandwiches at home. Instead she just put food in a basket— Portuguese bread, a chunk of cheese, some links of chorizo, fruit, and tomatoes. At this picnic with Mary Grand and Dwight, she opened a can of sardines and fished them out with her fingers. She tore off pieces of Portuguese bread for Penny and Blair and me. Then she took a tomato and pulled it apart with her thumbs. The juice ran all over her fingers and dripped on her thighs. I was revolted and refused the half tomato that she offered. It seemed so selfish of her to stick her fingers into food that she expected someone else to eat.

Dwight Macdonald holding a
seagull. My dog Chata is
behind him, 1951

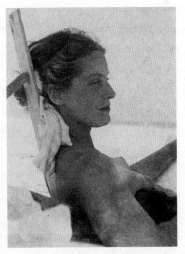

My mother with her dog,
Cape Cod, 1936

About once a week we had nighttime beach picnics to which everyone came from our pond area, which we called the "back woods." There were friends from the bay side in Wellfleet as well. We made a fire and cooked hamburgers and frankfurters and marshmallows. As it grew dark and the fire lapsed into embers, we sang. The person who led the singing was David Chavchavadze, a handsome man at least ten years older than the oldest of us. David was the son of my parents' friends, Nina and Paul Chavchavadze, who lived in South Wellfleet. Paul was a Georgian-Russian prince, Nina a Russian princess, a Romanov. Exiled from their country, the Chavchavadzes made do, and lived like the rest of us, a little bit from hand-to-mouth. David Chavchavadze knew songs in English, French, and Russian. Blair sang with him. She knew how to harmonize. Those of us who knew the lyrics joined in. Someone would go off in the dark to fetch more kindling for the fire, and we sat like spokes on a wheel with our feet near the flames to keep them warm. I loved the fact that our bundled-up bodies were invisible. All you saw was faces flushed with the glow of the fire.

Serge Chermayeff's youngest son, Peter, then a student at Phillips Andover, came to most of the picnics. He had a beautiful speaking voice with a hint of an English accent, and when he smiled, he looked so tender. I had a crush on Peter, so I tried not to look at him. Once, Peter sat next to me at a beach picnic. He didn't sit there because of me. It was just a good place for him to get near the fire. His arm was about four inches from my shoulder, and I felt like putting my shoulder against his, but of course I would never do anything like that. I couldn't even sing when he was beside me. I was afraid that my voice would crack. I could sing best when I was next to Blair and could copy her notes and timing. Her voice drowned mine out, and that was the way I wanted it.

Closer to my age were Charlie Jencks, Mike Macdonald, and Reuel Wilson. We all referred to them as if it were one word:

"CharlieMikeandReuel." They ignored me except when my beautiful friend Grania Gurievitch came to visit. She looked older than me, and she was thin with glossy brown hair and a mischievous smile. Her high-pitched voice and English accent were perfect for flirting. I tried to copy Grania's intonation, but it felt fake, so I stopped.

I had known Grania from infancy. Every Christmas we went to her mother Nemone's caroling party and I spent many nights in Grania's family's wooden house in Manhattan's East Nineties. I had envied Grania for having an Austrian housekeeper-nanny who made quarter-moon-shaped cookies dusted with powdered sugar. A plate of these cookies would be waiting for Grania when she came home from the Brearley School. Since Grania was skinny, she could eat as many cookies as she wanted. This Austrian woman loved Grania, which was good, because Grania's mother, Nemone, was a manic depressive and sometimes was so sad and helpless that Grania had to tie her shoelaces. In Grania's childhood bedroom, expensive toys were neatly arranged on shelves. When we were about six, we traded toys. I cannot remember what I gave Grania, but I treasured what she gave me—a small book about bears, its covers lined with real fur. I always felt guilty that I had gotten the better deal.

Coche de Mama

Every year autumn announces itself too early. In mid-August a few branches of the tupelo trees along the pond's edge turn red, and the tops and bottoms of the reeds lining the shore become yellow. Seeing that red and yellow fills me with dread. Crows flap from tree to tree, first they go *caw*, *caw*, *caw*, then they make four *caws* and finally a steady *caw* noise reverberates in the forest like a chain saw. Their squawks foretell winter darkness and loss. With summer over, Blair and I always have to leave our pond. This means leaving either our mother or our father or both.

In September 1950, our father was on the Cape checking on his rental properties. For a few weeks, Blair and I lived at the Turkey Houses just with him, and we vied to get his attention and to make him happy. It felt like an extra piece of summer even though the turkey cabins had become chilly at night, and my nose and hands got cold if they were outside of the blankets. This was the time of year when, by half past three, the sun was gone from the beach in front of our porch, and you had to swim almost to the middle of the pond to be in the sun.

One morning, when our father had gone to Orleans to buy something for one of his houses, our mother turned up at the bottom of the Turkey Houses driveway. When she opened her car door, she looked angry. Maybe she always looked angry when she was tense. After kissing Blair and me, she stepped back to give us her appraising look (to see if we were fatter or thinner, prettier or

My mother arriving at the Turkey Houses in
the Coche de Mama, 1950

uglier). She then announced that she had a new secondhand station wagon. "This is the Coche de Mama," she said. "We are going
to Mexico." The car was a huge Chrysler with real wood paneling
on the outside. In the back she had packed her belongings—her
paints, her folding easel, and a duffle bag with clothes. All of this
was covered with a mattress. She reached into the front seat and
handed us each a little wooden lacquer-covered box hinged at the
back like a sailor's trunk. Mine was black, decorated with blue and
pink flowers. Blair's was red, decorated with exotic birds. We would
take these with us, our mother said. "In Mexico you can buy silver
jewelry for almost nothing. These can be your jewelry boxes."

    Blair and I had not spent much time with our mother since
the fall of 1948 when, after putting us on a train to go to boarding
school in Vermont, she drove to Mexico to get a divorce. Then I
was almost eight. Now I was almost ten. Blair was three and a half

years older. Whenever our mother did turn up, she brought presents from Mexico, animals made of clay or embroidered blouses for Blair and me. She always made everything sound wonderful. She was like sunshine. Blair and I moved toward her like two Icaruses, but we never touched her golden rays.

From the back of the car, she pulled two duffle bags, carried them into our turkey cabins, and helped us pack. All we had was shorts, blue jeans, T-shirts, and bathing suits, plus a couple of sweaters, and, of course, underwear. Blair looked pensive. "What about Daddy?" she asked. "Anna will tell him where you have gone," our mother said. Anna Matson and my mother confided in each other. They talked about their lovers and husbands and about their experience of sex—things they never told their children. Our mother surveyed our clothes laid out on our beds. "Don't you have any proper shoes?" she asked. All I had was worn-out sneakers with holes near my little toes. We had gone barefoot most of the summer, and I was proud that my feet were tough enough to walk barefoot in the town of Wellfleet even when the sidewalks were hot. The occasional stick on the path to the ocean didn't bother me. The only painful thing was when the squirrels broke up the pine cones and scattered prickly pieces on our pine needle paths.

Our mother drove Blair and me to Provincetown, parked on MacMillan Wharf, and led us across the street to the New York Store, the only store in town that had everything. It was full of back-to-school supplies. We found the aisle for shoes and socks and our mother bought brown lace-up Oxfords for me and a pair of loafers for Blair. She gave Blair two dimes to put in the slots over the loafers' arch. I wished I were old enough to wear loafers. My mother thought that to wear them you had to be at least twelve. I loved it when my mother bought me things—anything, even just an ice cream cone or a Little Lulu comic book. Instead of being hurt or angry that she had gone to live in Mexico without us, I was grateful that she had come to get us.

After shopping, we had club sandwiches at the Mayflower Café. The place was dark and smelled of alcohol. For me that smell went with the pleasure of going to a restaurant intended for adults only. There was a big brown wooden bar with men sitting on stools. The walls were lined with cartoon drawings of Provincetown characters. My favorite was three-hundred-and-fifty-pound Fat Francis, who used to walk up and down Commercial Street wearing a tuxedo and a top hat. There were cartoons of two handsome Portuguese fishermen that my mother and her women friends thought were "divine." One of them, Herman Tasha, gave my mother fresh fish whenever she asked for it, and every year he took us out on his boat for the Blessing of the Fleet. Kaki Captiva was not quite as good-looking as Herman, but he was equally virile. He caused a crisis when Dodie, Jack Hall's first wife, fell in love with him, divorced Jack, and went off with Kaki to live in the south.

Back at the Turkey Houses, our mother stuffed our packed duffle bags under the mattress in the back of the Coche de Mama. Anna Matson came to say good-bye. It felt funny not saying good-bye to my father. Anna promised to give him hugs and kisses from Blair and me. The casual way Anna and my mother talked made me feel there was nothing unusual about leaving the Cape and driving to Mexico. Blair and I had a last swim. The pond was colder than it had been a week earlier. A gust of wind chased ripples hither and yon. I loved my body when it was submerged in water. No one could see it, but I could feel every part of it because water touched me everywhere. We dried ourselves, dressed on the sandy shore, and walked up to the Coche de Mama. I looked back at the pond one last time. There were still water lilies floating among the lily pads and, closer to shore, light caught the tops of the ripples making them look like black and silver stripes. I wished I could hug the pond. Once I took a jar of Horseleech Pond water with me when I left in the fall. But it was pointless. After a week, I threw the water away. If we had waited an hour, pink clouds would have bobbed up and down on the water's surface, and if we had waited even longer, a path of light would have led across the water to the rising moon.

Our mother slid onto the big maroon-color leather front seat. Her hands on the Bakelite steering wheel looked so competent. Blair and I crawled into the back of the Coche de Mama and sat on top of the mattress, which would be our home for the whole week that it took to drive to Mexico City.

I liked the idea of Mexico. I had seen pictures of it in children's books—dancing girls in *China Poblana* costumes. They wore long red skirts dotted with sequins and white puff-sleeved blouses embroidered with flowers. Around their shoulders was a *rebozo* and around their necks, multiple necklaces of shiny colored beads like miniature Christmas tree balls. Their hair was done up in braids that were sometimes looped up and fastened with big bows. If the book was about a boy, he might be sitting by a cactus or riding a donkey. Mexican boys in children's books always wore sombreros. In the Coche de Mama, our mother kept telling us how beautiful Mexico was—the flowers, the mountains, the pink, blue, and yellow houses behind whose walls lay turquoise swimming pools.

Our road trip took us south through Massachusetts, Rhode Island, Connecticut, New York, Pennsylvania, Maryland, Virginia, Tennessee, Georgia, Alabama, Mississippi, Louisiana, and Texas—farther and farther from our father, farther and farther from our father's pond. By the side of the road in Louisiana I caught sight of turtles resting on a log half sunk on the shore of a slow-moving river. My whole body went into catch mode. I wanted to run down to the riverbank and scoop the turtles up, but my mother was in a hurry to get to Mexico. I could picture the way Horseleech Pond must have looked right then—its silver ripples lifting the edge of a lily pad and then rolling through pickerel reeds until they disappeared upon the shore. At this exact minute, a little black turtle head might be poking up between the lily pads. There were still so many to catch. The Coche de Mama kept moving south. Enormous trees by the side of the road were hung with Spanish moss. It looked like mistletoe. I tried to look at the trees and to not think about Cape Cod. Our mother was being a real mother. She really wanted us to live with her in Mexico.

We stopped for lunch at a drugstore that had a soda fountain. In front of the counter was a line of high stools with round leatherette seats. Our mother ordered hamburgers, and Blair and I asked for milkshakes. On the wall above the grill was a sign that said that only white people could sit at the counter. I was enraged. Gaga had taught Blair and me that discrimination was wrong. Our mother admired black people. Hers was, however, an admiration that focused on how beautiful they were and how different they were from us. I felt like remonstrating with the waitress but, with her bouncy ponytail and her clean white apron, she looked like a nice person, and I thought maybe it was not her fault. After seeing that sign in Louisiana, I did not like the South. I don't think the southerners liked us either. They could tell from our accents that we were northerners, and since we were on our way to Mexico, they probably thought we were communists.

Sometimes Blair and I got to sit beside our mother in the front seat. I loved to watch my mother drive. I liked the firm way her hands held the wheel, the little movements left and right as she steered. The line from her forehead to her chin was as beautiful as a movie star. Her nose had a curve like a bow that made her look as if she were always pointing forward.

Our mother was a brave driver. She seemed to know exactly where she was going, and pretty soon we were in Texas, an unending expanse of cracked earth punctuated by olive-brown cacti.

No matter where you looked, nothing was really green. I missed the bright green lawns of New England. "Do you already have a house?" Blair asked. "No," my mother said. She hoped to find a house with a garden and a pool.

The reason she had decided to keep on living in Mexico was that she was in love with a Mexican man named Edmundo Lassalle. He had almost pure Indian blood, she said, and when he was young, he had been a spy and had married an Austrian princess. He was handsome. We would like him. As we drove south, Blair composed a ballad about this romantic figure. Every day she invented new verses that went with the tune of "The Streets of Laredo," a ballad we both knew. The closer we got to Mexico City, the more excited we were about meeting Edmundo.

The road in Texas was a straight line all the way to the horizon. When I got bored, I tried to count the sections of yellow line in the middle of the road. Most of the time we went so fast that the lines vanished under the hood of the car before I could count them. I liked it better when the yellow line was unbroken. It's more peaceful. Everything in front and everything behind is just one path and you are not sure whether you are seeing the same piece of yellow line over and over, or whether at each moment the line is new. It must be a lonely job to paint such a line. My mother told me they do it at night when there are no cars on the road. I pictured a lonely line painter dragging his paint pail from town to town.

Sometimes I counted telephone poles. The spaces between them were tiny when the poles were far ahead of us, and they became wider and wider until we were beside them. Space keeps changing. Nothing is fixed. In the far distance, I saw water in the middle of the road. Maybe there is an oasis in this desert, I thought. But when we got to where the puddle had been, the road was dry. "It's a mirage," my mother explained. "The heat causes mirages." After that I kept my eyes on the farthest point in the road, trying to see a mirage as long as I could before it vanished. For a while the mirages seemed miraculous, but later they became humdrum. Something else to watch out for on the hot, flat tarmac was a kind of bird that my mother called a roadrunner. These birds were about the size of a small chicken, and they would dash out of the brush and cross the road in front of us.

The road's endlessness was unnerving, especially the time when my mother thought we might run out of gas. Luckily, she had a canteen full of water, so if we broke down, we would not die of thirst. Still, I dreaded being stuck on the side of the road. No cars went by. We could be stranded for hours and hours, even days, and we had no food. A truck might come along and give us a lift to the nearest town, but a truck in Texas was bound to have some kind of beer-glugging gunslinger at the wheel. We did not run out of gas. A black rectangle appeared on the horizon. It was not a mirage; it was a filling station. We stopped, filled the tank, and bought some cold drinks, a loaf of bread, and jars of peanut butter and jelly for a picnic.

We had driven halfway through Texas when our mother suddenly pulled off the road. The Coche de Mama was boiling over. She raised the hood to let the engine cool before opening the radiator cap to pour water in it. Then she announced, "I'm hungry, aren't you?" Without waiting for an answer, she said, "This looks like a perfect place for a picnic." I did not see anything perfect about it. Everything in Texas was dust-colored, and there were no shade trees, just dry scrub. Our mother led us down a narrow path that she was convinced would lead to a river. To me it looked like the kind of path that might lead to an open area littered with toilet paper. She forged ahead carrying a bag of food. Blair and I followed, walking slowly to demonstrate our reluctance. My feet kicked up clouds of dust that settled between my toes because I was wearing sandals.

About fifteen feet ahead of us our mother stopped. "Oh!" she exclaimed. "There is a baby rattlesnake right in the path!" Her voice sounded more intrigued than alarmed. A second later we watched her step over the snake. Blair and I stayed where we were scanning the bushes to see if there were any more snakes. "It's just a baby rattlesnake. It's quite sweet, all curled up. Come see." We took a few steps toward our mother. Baby or not, I knew the snake could kill us. My mother's attitude annoyed me. She was fearless, so I had to be afraid for her. Finally, the snake slithered into the bushes and Blair and I caught up with our mother. We sat in the scratchy grass while our mother spread peanut butter and jelly on Tip Top bread—all that had been available at the filling station's convenience store. "Disgusting!" she said. "Americans do not know how to make bread." I didn't tell her that soft white sliced bread was my favorite.

After sundown, our mother checked into a seedy-looking motel, and we had skinny gray hamburgers in a nearby diner. That night, the night after the snake picnic, I couldn't sleep. People in the motel parking lot kept getting into and out of cars. There were loud voices and slamming doors. I was afraid someone might come near and see us lying in the car under a sheet. Even with the Coche de Mama's windows open, it was hot. I had to keep turning my pillow around to find a place that wasn't wet from perspiration. Another problem was that Blair and I argued over where the middle of the mattress was; Blair always trespassed on my side. Now that she was a teenager, she thought she had special rights.

The following morning our mother checked out of the motel room early and started driving while Blair and I were still half asleep in the back of the car. After about an hour we woke up and the Coche de Mama was moving through the middle of a town. "Keep your eyes peeled for a good breakfast place," our mother said. I scanned the right side of the street and Blair scanned the left. A few minutes later we saw smoke billowing out of the Coche de Mama's hood. It smelled acrid. Our mother stopped the car and told us to get out. I could tell she was trying to keep her voice calm, but she sounded angry. We did not want to get out because we were still in our pajamas and there were people on the sidewalk. My pajamas were so old that you could see my body through the thin cloth. When our mother warned us that the car might explode, we climbed out and stood on the hot sidewalk in our bare feet. People gathered around but they didn't pay attention to Blair and me. Their eyes were focused on the burning engine. Our mother acted as if this were just another adventure.

Someone came and put some liquid on the fire and the smoke stopped. By the time a fire engine arrived the fire was out. Our mother was given the name of a mechanic who could put in a new engine or fix the old one. Blair and I got dressed in the back of the car, and a tow truck dragged the Coche de Mama to a garage. While the mechanic inspected the car's engine, Blair and I sat on a pile of tires and played double solitaire. It was boiling hot. When water splashed on the tar, the puddle evaporated in five seconds. We had breakfast in that town and lunch, too. To kill time while waiting for the Coche de Mama to be repaired, we went to the five and ten cent store and bought a carrot peeler and a can opener for my mother and art supplies for Blair and me. After that, our mother dropped us at a movie house where we saw *The Black Rose*, with Tyrone Power and Orson Welles. When the engine was fixed, our mother had barely enough money to pay for it. We would have to be extra careful about money until we got to Mexico City, she said.

Our mother had planned to cross the border at Laredo, but at the last minute she headed to Brownsville instead. Because of the fire we arrived at the border after dark and the border control office was closed. When she saw the darkened glass-enclosed customs office on the American side of the bridge over the Rio Grande, she said, "I'm going through." At the very top of the bridge she stopped. Blair and I got out of the car and put one foot in the United States and the other in Mexico. It was like being two people at once. As we passed the shuttered customs office on the Mexican side of the bridge and drove down into Mexico, I looked back to see if any police cars were following us. Policemen scared me. They always look at you as if you have done something wrong. Maybe our father thought we had been kidnapped and had told the border police not to let us into Mexico. Our mother was quiet. When I asked her questions, she just answered yes, no, or *mmm*. Her eyes never left the road. I wanted to chat with her since we were now outlaws. If something bad happened to us in Mexico, no one would ever know. Our father would never find us. We might never see our pond again. Our mother must have had misgivings, too, because after about forty-five minutes she made a U-turn and headed back to the Rio Grande.

We crossed the bridge to the American side of the border and spent the night in a cheap hotel. Because we were in a town, Blair and I were allowed to sleep on cots in our mother's room instead of in the back of the Coche de Mama. The room was dirty, the kind of dirt you cannot see, but you know it is ground into the bedspread and carpet so that you wish you had slippers to wear to get to the bathroom.

The next morning, we had pancakes. "Our last American breakfast," our mother observed. At the border control office, I was afraid that they would somehow know that we had sped out of our country the night before. But the men in uniforms on both sides of the bridge treated us as ordinary sightseers on our way to Mexico. They stamped our tourist cards and waved us on. "We'll see you in six months," said a young officer. Tourist cards were good for only half a year. "Yes, until then," my mother said.

21

Mexico

On the Mexican side of the Rio Grande everything changed. The houses were low and painted in pastel colors. Windows were dark openings. Old men sat in doorways. Women carried heavy bundles. Younger men stood around leaning against the wall outside of a bar—a cantina, my mother called it. Women were not welcome in there. The dogs in Mexico were skinny and wore no collars because they didn't belong to anyone. The side streets were unpaved, and the main street was full of holes. It was lined with food vendors, women with dark cotton shawls over their heads kept fires going in low, square tin stoves. Small children squatted near their mothers. Their clothes were worn and skimpy. One small boy was dressed in only a dirty undershirt. When my mother stopped the car near one of the food vendors, a group of children about my age and younger gathered at the window crying *"Chicles! Chicles!"* They held up boxes containing Chiclets. To my astonishment, I heard my mother talking to them in Spanish. She had learned it during her two years in Mexico. Even though she thought gum chewing was vulgar, to be nice, she bought four Chiclets, two in little red boxes, two in yellow. The boy who sold them to us turned away as soon as she gave him his money.

What our mother really wanted was Mexican food. She found a woman selling tamales. I was wary—the food might be full of germs. My mother said that the charcoal fire burned all the germs away. Some tamales were sweet, she said, and some were hot. I asked for a sweet one. You can tell which are the sweet tamales because the corn husks in which they are wrapped have a pink stain on them. Hot tamales usually have a spot of reddish brown. She showed us how to partly unwrap our tamales and to use the corn husk to hold the warm grainy patty inside. The tamale was my first taste of Mexican food. To my relief, it was like cream of wheat, but more succulent.

For the next two days we drove south through mountains. When I wanted to stop and find a bush behind which to pee, my mother told me that in this part of Mexico it was dangerous to stop just anywhere. Bandits wielding machetes could descend from the hills. They would be happy to kill us in order to steal the Coche de Mama. I looked up and pictured bands of men brandishing knives racing down the steep slope.

Much to my annoyance, my mother carried on about the beauty of the mountains and valleys, the jacaranda trees with lavender blossoms and no leaves, the majestic *ahuehuetes* (also called Montezuma bald cypress), the cacti, and especially the Indians. In a narrow valley on the right side of the road she spotted men following mules pulling a plow. The field-workers—she called them *campesinos*—wore simple white pants and shirts made out of a heavy cotton called *manta*. "These people have been doing the same work the same way for centuries," she observed. "It is so much more beautiful than the way farmers work in the United States with their ugly machines. Here people and the earth follow the same rhythm." Our mother pointed out that the field-workers' postures were exactly like the postures of Indians tilling the soil in Diego Rivera's murals. She had met Rivera at a party and found him amusing. His wife, Frida Kahlo, she saw as a little overblown. "I will take you to see Rivera's murals in the Cortez Palace in Cuernavaca. Cuernavaca is a beautiful town an hour south of Mexico City. That's where I hope to find a house."

My mother extolled all things handmade. She despised machines. She admired the mud brick houses with tin roofs held down by rocks. Some of them had metal Pepsi-Cola signs stuck on their front walls, but that didn't mean that you could buy Pepsi there. She loved Mexican open-air markets where the women selling food sit on the ground. To her a market was a visual splendor. In one of the cities that we drove through, probably Morelia, she took Blair and me to a market and bought odd-looking fruits as well as regular-looking bananas. There were also some miniature bananas that she insisted we taste. They had a stronger perfume than standard American bananas. After that they were my fruit of choice. A banana peel is a good thing—no germs can get at the part you eat. In the craft section of the market she bought us woolen ribbons in bright colors. "Now that you are in Mexico you can braid these into your hair."

Just as we were making our way back to the car, an old man selling puppets approached us. At first my mother shook her head and said, "No, *gracias.*" The man gently jiggled a wooden structure from which about fifteen puppets dangled. Their heads were made of papier-mâché and each one had differently painted features. Even though my mother kept saying no, the man demonstrated how he could make a puppet dance. "Cantinflas!" he said. My mother explained that the puppet looked like a cartoon of Mexico's famous comic movie actor. I wanted a puppet, but I didn't ask. Blair was braver: "Let's get two and we can make up plays with them." Our mother relented. I chose a girl puppet wearing a *China Poblana* costume, and Blair chose a male puppet with a little straw hat and a brown poncho folded over one shoulder. For the rest of the afternoon, sitting on the mattress in the back of the Coche de Mama, Blair and I invented dialogues for our puppets. The strings of my puppet kept getting tangled. I tried not to cry. Failure made me furious. After saying, "Fix it yourself" for a long while, Blair helped me untangle the mess.

As we entered the Valley of Mexico, the fields became fewer and the houses closer and closer together. The outskirts of Mexico City, like the outskirts of New York City, looked forlorn. I tried to imagine what it would be like to live in such a place. What if both my parents died and I landed on the edge of a city where I didn't know anyone—how would I survive? After a while the houses became like one big house. Their front walls were all attached to one another. The way you could tell the houses apart was when they switched from blue, to ochre, or to a dark rusty pink. As the sun went down, the walls lost their brightness. My mother turned right onto a tree-lined avenue that took us to a big plaza with a bandstand in the middle. "This part of Mexico City is called Coyoacán," she said. "And this is Coyoacán's central plaza. See, the church over there? It's one of the oldest in Mexico."

Our mother told us that we were going to Pepita's house. "It's just a couple of blocks from here." Pepita was Edmundo's mother, she said. Actually, she was his aunt. Edmundo was an orphan, and Pepita had looked after him, but our mother did not tell us this until later. We turned down a side street, and dust billowed up all around the Coche de Mama. I watched dust particles turning somersaults in the halo of light around a streetlamp.

22

Coyoacán

The Coche de Mama stopped in front of a tall, white wall with a green metal gate. My mother got out and pulled on a loop of wire that came through a hole in the wall to the right of the gate. A bell rang somewhere inside. After what seemed a very long wait, an old woman not even as tall as me and dressed all in black opened the gate. My mother gave her a hug and told us to get out of the car and to come and meet Pepita. "What you say is '*Mucho gusto!*'" my mother advised. Pepita patted Blair and me on the shoulder and said something in Spanish. "She says you are welcome to her house," my mother said.

Pepita's house was just one room leading to another with no hallway. Each room had a door leading out to a paved patio. The rooms had high ceilings and almost no windows. The room farthest from the entrance was the kitchen, and here we sat at a heavy wooden table while Pepita served us corn soup and hot tortillas with salt and butter. "Mexicans don't usually use butter," my mother said. "Pepita is giving you butter because she knows that American girls like it. Usually you just put a little salt on a tortilla and roll it up."

After supper we followed Pepita and our mother back through the string of rooms to a room that was to be Blair's and my bedroom. It was stark with just two beds, a huge dark wooden armoire for a closet, and a tall bureau whose top was covered with a lace doily. Hanging over one bed was a crucifix, over the other a small print of the Virgin of Guadalupe. Our mother sat with us while we changed into pajamas. Then she leaned over our beds and kissed us good night. She told us that Pepita was going to take care of us for a little while. Blair and I begged her not to go. Pepita would be lots of fun, our mother said, and she was a good cook. She could make wonderful Mexican desserts. And Pepita could teach us Spanish. I hated it when my mother sounded fake jolly. When she was like that I could never get her to change her mind. We knew our mother was going off to see Edmundo, and she wanted to be with Edmundo alone. She would be back soon, in just a few days, she promised. *"Buenas noches,"* she said as she went out the door. I heard the Coche de Mama's engine starting up and I pictured my mother at the wheel, driving through the city to see her lover. I was sad: she wanted to be with him, not us. She loved him more. Well, she was in love. Still, I felt dumped.

Our bedroom had no bedside tables, so there were no bedside lamps to read by. Either Blair or I had to get out of bed to turn off the light—a single bulb hanging from the middle of the ceiling. The light switch was by the door and closest to my bed, so Blair said it was my job to turn off the light. I hated scrambling back to bed in the dark. "Tomorrow night it's your turn," I said. I had Buttoneyes, my musical brown bear next to me. He was the only one of my fuzzy animals that I had been allowed to keep when we left New York for boarding school two years earlier. I wound his music box up over and over until I felt sleepy. When you stop winding, the music gets slower and slower as if the bear were falling asleep, too.

Early the following morning I woke up to a rooster's crow. At first, I didn't know where I was, but then I saw Buttoneyes on the floor with his brass music box winder sticking out of his back. And there on a chair were the clothes I took off before I put on my pajamas. Yes, I was at Pepita's house. She was the brown-skinned old lady who didn't speak English and who gave us soup. I looked at the bedroom's high, white ceiling and remembered the lights of the Coche de Mama, zigzagging across our walls, widening into a triangle, then narrowing to a thin straight beam that dashed across the ceiling and was gone.

Blair was lying on her back reading. She didn't notice that I was awake, so I just closed my eyes and tried to think of nothing. "I know you're awake," Blair said. "I can tell from your breathing. Come on, let's get up and have breakfast." Neither of us knew where Pepita's bedroom was, so we retraced our steps from the night before and found our way back to the kitchen. Here we discovered steps that led down to a yard. Beneath a gigantic black walnut tree there were about ten chickens plus a rooster scratching in the dry earth. I gathered a bunch of fallen walnuts, but I could not figure out how to get the nut out of its prickly casing.

Pepita appeared at the kitchen door. "*Buenos días!*" she called. "*Buenos días!*" we replied. I was beginning to think I knew a lot of Spanish. Pepita signaled for us to come up the kitchen steps, and she showed us a storeroom where she kept a pail of dried corn nuggets for the chickens. She gave us each a little bowl to fill with corn to scatter on the ground. The corn kernels felt silky as they slipped through my fingers. Soon I was surrounded by chickens pecking near my feet. I wished I could pat them the way I had patted my mother's New York cats, but the chickens moved away if I touched them.

We spent the next days in Pepita's dark, mostly unused rooms. There was a formal dining room, with a cupboard with glass doors behind which was crystal and porcelain—things that had not been touched in years. We only went into Pepita's bedroom once. Her walls were hung with religious images. On her bureau were old framed photographs—some of Edmundo as a boy and several of a dark-skinned man who must have been Pepita's husband. There was a wedding photograph. Pepita, now so shriveled, had once been beautiful. How unfair to be young and then to be old. I felt the same way about Gaga's wrinkly arms and her age-spotted hands with their raised blue veins. It seemed odd to me that old people could be so cheerful when every part of their bodies was shriveling. I wondered if, when I got old, would I mind the way the flesh on my arms sagged and jiggled.

Pepita's house had bookshelves filled with dusty leather-bound volumes, the kind in which the paper is so dry it cracks as you turn the pages. Luckily, our mother had made sure we had books. She had bought us each a pile of books for our journey south, and since I was such a slow reader, there were two I still had not read. Every day we fed the chickens. There was a wall at the bottom of the garden, which I knew I could climb over, but I always stopped partway up. On the other side of the wall was more brown earth covered with dusty, dried-up leaves and a few banana trees on a long downward slope, the bottom of which I could not see. Maybe there was a stream down there. Looking over the wall was seeing another world, a piece of land that could join me to the whole world if I dared to step into it. I imagined going there and walking and walking in strange empty places, walking and walking until I was not myself anymore.

Pepita spoke to us in Spanish, which we did not understand. She was kind and did not expect us to answer her. She cooked our meals and washed our dishes. We ate a lot of eggs, rice, and beans. She made a custard called flan for dessert. I thought she must be lonely living alone in that many-roomed house. Maybe she liked having two American girls come to stay.

When our mother came to see us a few days later, there was a new gold bracelet on her wrist, and she was wearing a blue dress I'd never seen before. We walked a few blocks to Coyoacán's Plaza Centenario, on the far side of which was a shop sign that said *Panadería*. In the store's window were heaps of pastries. "Take a tray," our mother said, "and take tongs to pick them up with. You can have what you like, just make sure to add four *bolillos*—see those little bread rolls to the left of the cash register? I will take four of them home for Edmundo's and my supper." Blair and I each picked up a round metal tray from a stack near the shop's entrance and we went around the store choosing *pan dulces*. The saleswoman added up the bill. Most pastries cost a peso. Some of the fancier ones with custard inside cost more, but our mother warned us to avoid anything with custard. It might have bacteria. The saleswoman made two packages out of square white papers whose corners she folded toward the middle and then twisted and tied with a thin red string. The butter from the pastries turned parts of the paper translucent.

Blair and I carried our packages across the street, and our mother carried a bag of *bolillos*. We sat on a bench in the plaza and sampled our purchases. There were three kinds of pastry that would remain my favorites for many years. The best were *orejas*, meaning ears. They were shaped like hearts or butterflies. Our mother said that in France they were called *palmiers*, because they resembled palm leaves. The next best was a sugar-sprinkled *churro*. These were about as long as a banana and ridged like a fluted column. The third type that I liked a lot was a thick sugar cookie. They were heavy. You couldn't eat more than one. Some *pan dulces* were more like buns with a coating of beige-colored sugar on the top. They were boring. My mother assured me that they would be good for breakfast with butter and honey.

From the plaza we walked to an adjacent park to rent bicycles. I had learned to ride a bicycle in Cornwall, but I was not sure that I remembered how. Blair sped off on her bike while our mother held on to the back of my bicycle seat until I got my balance. She was being so nice. This was not the kind of thing she liked to do. I was happy. After that I rode around and around on the paved paths that circumvented flowerbeds, feeling like a champion. I hoped my mother was watching. I wanted her to be proud of me. When the hour's rental was up, we returned the bicycles and, on the way out of the park we stopped at an ice cream cart. The owner opened the top and we surveyed the vats of pink, orange, and yellow sherbet. The cart also sold *paletas*, popsicles, and our mother bought those for us because she said they were probably made with purified water, whereas the sherbet might not be. Sucking on popsicles, we returned to Pepita's house. When we reached the green gate, our mother opened the tailgate of the Coche de Mama and took out four books that she had borrowed from the Benjamin Franklin Library, which had English-language books. Two were for me and two for Blair. For me she had a Nancy Drew mystery and *The Secret Garden*, which became my favorite novel. For Blair she had *The Call of the Wild* and some other book.

Late one afternoon our mother turned up and drove us to the middle of Mexico City. We followed wide avenues, one called Insurgentes and another called Paseo de la Reforma. The Reforma was magnificent, much grander than New York's Park Avenue. Every few blocks there was a roundabout (my mother called it a *glorieta*) in the center of which was a statue. The three statues I liked best were of a horse (the Caballito, my mother explained); Diana, a naked woman with a bow; and the third was a golden angel on top of a tall pole. "We're going to have supper with Edmundo," our mother said. She parked near a tall, modern apartment building near Chapultepec Park, and we went up in the elevator to a high floor. She rang the bell even though she had the keys in her hand. Edmundo came to the door. He was over six feet tall and he had slicked-back black hair. I think he oiled it because you could see the channels where the comb ran through it. He was wearing a *guayabera*, a starched white shirt with two lines of narrow pleats running down the front and back. He smelled good, some kind of cologne, probably expensive. He had a big smile as he leaned down and gave Blair and me each a hug. "Beautiful girls!" he exclaimed to our mother. "What marvelous girls you have!" So, he liked us. That was good.

He led us into his living room, took bottles of Coca-Cola out of a small refrigerator, and gave us each one. He and our mother drank tequila. There was a bowl of salted peanuts on the coffee table, and he told us we were welcome to eat them. A maid served dinner in the dining room: *filete* (steak), potatoes, and zucchini— nothing problematic. And there were tortillas instead of bread. Edmundo told us that even though he never brushed his teeth, he had never had a cavity because he ate tortillas. Indeed, his teeth were extremely white. They were even, too. He and our mother chatted about friends, art exhibitions (he had helped my mother find a gallery to show her paintings the year before), and possible houses to rent. Edmundo told all kinds of funny stories. He laughed a lot, a hilarious high-pitched laugh, almost like a mariachi singer's wail. He made us giggle. And he really was handsome, just as our mother had said.

Edmundo Lassalle

23

Cuernavaca

After another week of our living at Pepita's, our mother returned. "I've found a house!" she said. "It has a swimming pool. You are going to love it!" We said good-bye and *"Muchas gracias"* to Pepita, who seemed sad to see us leave, climbed into the Coche de Mama, and headed south toward the range of mountains that lies between Mexico City and Cuernavaca. On the side of the road there were boys selling bunches of red carnations. We stopped and bought some. "For our new home," our mother said. At the top of the mountain were fields with long, yellow grasses blowing this way and that. Our mother pointed to a grove of pine trees on the left side of the car. "Over there is the perfect picnic spot," she said. "We'll come back up here soon." A minute later she pointed to the left again. "Look!" she cried. "You can see Popocatépetl! See that mountain covered with snow? That's a volcano. Maybe next weekend we can have a picnic near the snow." She told us that if we looked out the back window, we would see another volcano in the distance. It was long with two bumps instead of being shaped like a cone. "That's Iztaccíhuatl," she said. "Popo is said to be a warrior prince and Izta is a sleeping lady." Just before we started down the other side of the mountain and into the valley where the town of Cuernavaca (meaning cow's horn) lies, we stopped at Tres Marías, a village that consisted of a few huts and a line of charcoal braziers on which tamales and tacos were cooking. The tamales here were better than the ones we'd had in Brownsville. I ate three.

As we drove down the mountain, our mother honked the horn at the beginning of each curve. Mexican drivers, she explained, do not always stay on their side of the road. After a final hairpin turn that threw our bodies back and forth, we looked down on Cuernavaca. We entered the town through a gigantic white gate. After about half a mile of driving downhill, we turned right onto a side street lined with high walls in different colors. Our mother explained that behind the walls were houses and gardens. A few minutes later, the Coche de Mama stopped in front of a blue wall festooned with bougainvillea, some white and some magenta. Our mother had the key to the gate. It opened on to a garden so big that you couldn't tell where it ended. To the right was a low, dusty-pink one-story house with a veranda. Edmundo rented this for us, she said. He was an executive at Celanese, a company that made synthetic textiles, so he would have to work in Mexico City during the week. But he would join us in Cuernavaca on weekends.

We carried our bags into the house and dropped them in our bedroom, which had twin beds with matching bedspreads with fringed hems. I unpacked my books and put the unread ones on

Me and Blair on the veranda of the
Cuernavaca house, 1950

my bedside table. The house came with a cook and a maid. *"Mucho gusto,"* our mother reminded us to say. And, *"Cómo está usted?"* Our mother told the cook what to make for dinner. Except for when we visited Gaga or our great Aunt Martha, we had almost no experience with servants. Our mother appeared to be used to them. The way she told them what to do was different from the way Gaga talked to Annie and Bessie. Gaga spoke as if she were asking for a favor. Our mother made commands. And Gaga not only asked Blair and me to help clear the table, she also gave us detergent with which to wash our underpants. Even the Queen of England, she insisted, washed her own underwear. In Mexico, the maids did everything. They laundered, folded, and put away all our clothes, even Blair's new bra.

The next morning, our mother suggested a swim before breakfast. She led us across the lawn and through a group of enormous guava trees. The pungent smell of fallen and rotting guavas revolted me. I had to pick my way around squished fruits. The pool was green with algae. "It needs to be cleaned," my mother noted. "But there's no harm in green." She dove in. I climbed down the metal ladder and partway into the water. It smelled green. I was sure there were snakes in there, maybe lizards, too.

The maid, her name was Chavela, served breakfast on the veranda. *"Huevos revueltos y tocino,"* my mother said—scrambled eggs and bacon. *"Y pan tostado"* (toast). I looked at my mother as if I could tell by her face how she acquired this new sense of authority. When she was married to my father or to George Senseney, she did her own cooking and cleaning. During breakfast she taught Blair and me some Spanish words that we would need every day. Even though she couldn't sing, she taught us two Mexican songs— "Cielito Lindo" and "La Cucaracha," easy songs for children to learn. She took a long swallow of her coffee and then put her hands palms down on the table. "I've found a school for you," she said. "It's called Miss Heart's. It's an English school: Miss Heart is from

London and she has a beautiful speaking voice. She called last week and told me that she has a place for each of you."

After breakfast the next morning our mother led us downhill, past Cuernavaca's central plaza and to a building that looked more like a home than a school. She pushed open a heavy wooden door, and we followed her across a patio to Miss Heart's office. To me, Miss Heart, a delicate-looking woman with wavy white hair done up in a bun, looked old, but she was probably in her fifties. We shook her hand—I wondered if we were supposed to curtsy—and then she took me to a classroom with ten-year-olds and Blair to the third-form room. I was used to entering new schools well after the term had begun, but this was a foreign country and I didn't know what to expect. Miss Heart introduced me to my teacher. Then she turned to the class of about eight children, all seated behind wooden desks, and said, "Hayden Phillips has just arrived from the United States. She is going to join your class." The children nodded and murmured and stared. I was relieved when the teacher led me to a desk in the back row.

There was a red-haired boy at the desk next to mine. He was wearing shorts held up by suspenders, something I had only seen in children's books. He must be German or Austrian, I thought. He glanced at me and quickly turned his attention to the blackboard upon which the teacher was writing. After a while I realized that this was history class. It was the history of England about which I knew nothing. Next came math. At Miss Heart's, English and arithmetic were more advanced than at the Buckingham School. In English class we were reading Dickens's *A Tale of Two Cities*. It was long and hard with lots of words I did not know. We were told to look up new words in a dictionary and to keep a list of them in a notebook. We had a special book for vocabulary, and every week we learned at least forty new words. To me each new word was like a rung in a ladder: the more I knew, the more grown up I felt.

At the end of our first day at Miss Heart's, our mother picked us up. "I want you both to learn how to walk to and from school on your own. So, let's try to memorize the streets on our way home." The way home was simple: we followed a back street straight uphill for about half a mile. Blair made note of certain landmarks: "Okay, when we get to this red house we go left." I memorized a bar with swinging doors and then a coffin-making shop in whose dark interior I saw a stack of small white coffins for children. I was shocked: in the United States they always keep coffins hidden. Also, I didn't want to think about the little children that would die and that were the right size for these coffins.

About a block from our house we passed a building under construction. The workmen yelled things at Blair and me. "*Güerita!*" they cried, meaning little pale skinned blonde girl. I wasn't all that blonde and at nine years old, I was plump verging on fat, so I didn't see why they had to yell at me. They must have been yelling at thirteen-year-old Blair. She had bosoms. After keeping my eyes on the sidewalk for a couple of days, I decided to cross the street well before I reached the construction site. I still walked quickly and didn't look up. Blair thought I was being a baby. When the men shouted at her, she just threw her shoulders back and raised her chin a fraction of an inch. After about a month the catcalls didn't scare me anymore. My mother said they were harmless. But she did warn us never to look into the men's eyes. They would take that as an invitation.

On Saturday nights our mother and Edmundo took us to Cuernavaca's central plaza. At dusk the sky turns indigo blue and the leaves on the laurel trees turn black. "Listen," our mother said. "Listen to the laurels." Hidden in the leaves were masses of birds, all of them singing at the top of their lungs. On one side of the plaza the Cortez Palace was lit up. Our mother had taken us inside where, on the walls of an arcade, Diego Rivera's murals showed the Spaniards' cruelty to Indians. The most beautiful panel portrayed the *campesino* hero Zapata, dark and mustachioed, dressed in peasant white, and leading a white horse. He was the kind of man my mother liked, and I liked the looks of him, too.

Sunday night was the *paseo*. In an ornate hexagonal bandstand, musicians played Mexican music and the girls walked one way around the plaza and the boys walked in the opposite direction. That way we could look at one another. Blair and I wore our new three-tiered, blue-and-white striped skirts that our mother had bought for us at the Borda shop on the uphill side of the plaza. This skirt made me feel like a dancer. When I twirled, it went straight out. Remembering how Dasya's underpants showed when she twirled, I pinned my arms against my body to keep my skirt from flying up.

When we passed them, the Mexican boys looked at us but almost never approached us. There was one boy about my age that

Blair and me, in front of a street photographer's
screen, Central Plaza, Cuernavaca, 1950

I really liked. I could tell from the way he avoided my eyes that he liked the way I looked. Blair attracted more attention. She had tucked her blouse tight into her waistband to show off her new breasts. Sometimes she let the elasticized neckline of her blouse fall off one shoulder. She had beautiful shoulders—like a Greek statue. Her hair was pulled back in a ponytail. With her straight nose, narrow nostrils, and firm chin, she looked, our mother said, Junoesque. If we thought things were getting out of hand, if a boy came too near, we could always cross the street and sit with our mother and Edmundo who were drinking *copitas*, little glasses of tequila, at the outdoor café that was part of the Borda shop. Our mother never worried about us. Her attitude was that we could take care of ourselves, and we could.

After the band went home, Blair and I joined our mother and Edmundo at the café. Every few minutes a beggar approached our table. Some of them were mothers carrying infants wrapped tight in their *rebozos*, but most of the beggars were men and boys. The blind beggars frightened me. So did the ones whose skin looked as though they had leprosy. But the scariest one was a man with no legs who propelled himself around on a flat piece of wood with wheels. Edmundo warned us never to give the beggars anything. If you did, you would soon be surrounded by beggars. They pressed in close and touched you. Maybe they thought if they touched you, you would give them something just to make them go away. It was hard not to give money to the mothers with children, but we obeyed Edmundo and it soon became second nature to ignore beggars.

On Sunday mornings, Chavela brought us breakfast in bed. Around ten o'clock we would drive to the plaza and park on the street that led to the market. When we opened the car doors there were always a couple of small boys shouting *"Le cuido el coche?"* Our mother would nod to one of the boys and he would stand guard

next to the Coche de Mama. We followed our mother from stall to
stall as she priced fruits and vegetables with names like *sapote negro*
or jicama. The section of the market that had fly-covered meat
hanging from hooks smelled of blood that dripped onto the ground
and mixed with the water that had been used to wash the market's
cement floor in the morning. I hated getting that blood water on
my shoes. None of this bothered our mother. She bought a chicken
that to me looked slightly blue and insufficiently plucked. When
our mother's straw basket got heavy, she handed it to one of the
boys crowding around, all of them asking, *"Le ayudo?"* (Can I help
you?). Now she headed toward the flower stalls and bargained with
a fat woman to get a better price for a huge bunch of salmon-pink
gladiolas. She used to hate gladiolas—she thought they were com-
monplace, but since she had seen gladiolas in Diego Rivera's paintings of Indian women, she now saw them as typically Mexican. We
headed back to the Coche de Mama and our mother tipped first
the porter and then the car watcher, who, when he saw us coming,
made a great show of wiping the Coche de Mama's front window
with a filthy rag.

24

Outings

Cuernavaca was a happy town to live in. I liked Miss Heart's School, even though I was behind in math and even though I didn't make any friend to whom I felt close enough to invite home after school. No one invited me either. I was an overweight new girl—maybe that was the reason. Outside of school I did have one friend named Sandy Macpherson, whose widowed father, Cameron Macpherson, was a close friend of my mother's. The Macphersons lived in a huge house just downhill from the plaza. I loved going there. Sandy had a special girl's bedroom all done up with pink fabrics and eyelet lace. She even had a dressing table with her

Cameron Macpherson (right) beside his son, Christopher. His daughter, Sandy Macpherson, second from left, is flanked by a cousin and an unknown boy, c. 1950

Blair, Cuernavaca, 1950

matching comb and brush laid out on top. Sandy's father treated his daughter like a princess. I wondered if that was because she was adopted. She actually looked like a princess, delicate and fragile with white-blonde hair. Both of us were shy. We didn't talk much, but we were comfortable together. Each of us sensed, without putting words to it, a secret sadness in the other.

My mother asked Cam Macpherson, an amateur photographer, to take photographs of me and Blair. For the occasion, I wore my favorite dress, made of pink and gray plaid cotton and with a sash that tied in the back. Blair wore a low-cut dress with blue flowers printed all over it. Its waist was pulled in by rows of elastic thread that gathered up the cloth. For the posing session, Blair had curled her hair. She wasn't fat anymore. In the photograph she looks beautiful, a lot like our mother.

After Blair was done, I posed lying in the grass in front of a bed of nasturtiums. I tried to look grown up, like a movie star with my head propped on my hand. I had seen photographs of my mother posed this way. I put on a deep and thoughtful expression, which was hard, because the grass was itchy, and I was afraid that there might be a scorpion in the flowerbed. Cam kept putting his hand on my body in order to get me into the right position for the camera. It felt odd, but I did not dare say anything or move away. The photographs he took show a plump nine-year-old doing her best to look seductive.

After a while I began to feel part of the group at Miss Heart's School. I must have made a few friends because a photograph of my tenth birthday on November 20, 1950, shows me in our Cuernavaca garden with children who appear to be about my age. Four days after my birthday my father wrote Gaga that he had "glowing reports about Mexico from B & H as I gather you have. I miss them and I wish I could get a look at them from time to time." But he had a new baby to look at. He told his mother that his third daughter had been born five days earlier and they had named her Antonia.

The most confirming moment in terms of feeling part of a group was when, on some kind of national holiday (of which there were many in Mexico) our school joined all the Mexican schools in Cuernavaca in a parade. The band music made our marching seem

Me, Cuernavaca, 1950

My tenth birthday, me (center) and Blair (top right), in
our garden in Cuernavaca, November 1950

official and important. I had been told to wear red, white, and blue,
and my teacher gave me an American flag. Other foreign children
carried the flag of their countries. I was proud to be a flag bearer
and proud to be an American, even though most of the time I did
my best to look Mexican and even though my mother was always
saying that the United States was overrun with gas stations and
Howard Johnsonses.

My mother organized outings to places within driving distance
of Cuernavaca. Her favorite was Las Estacas, where we rented inner
tubes and floated down a river of yellowish green water that I got
used to even though it smelled like rotten eggs. The place I liked
the best was Palo Bolero, a pond fed by a waterfall that fell over the
mouth of a deep cave. Water pounded on our heads as we swam
into the cave. I never liked caves. Stalactites and stalagmites give me
the creeps, so I immediately turned back toward the light shining
through the wall of water that came down so fast it bounced when
it hit the pond's surface and made a roar that went right through my
skin. For me it was always a relief to swim out under the waterfall
and to see our mother standing near the shore in her two-piece red
hand-woven cotton bathing suit—she was the only woman there

My father and my sister Antonia,
Orgeval, France, 1950

with her midriff showing. Men kept looking at her. She seemed not to mind at all.

On the way home we usually stopped for supper at a fancy restaurant in a colonial hacienda. While my mother and Edmundo had their tequilas, Blair and I explored the roof of the partly ruined building. Descending the broad staircase that led to the dining room, I was reminded of movies with beautiful women in clingy evening gowns and white feather boas, stepping gracefully down grand staircases. My full skirt floated upward as I went down, and I pointed my toes outward and stepped quickly like a ballerina.

Our best trip was to Acapulco. Our mother and Edmundo drove there a few days before us to set up camp. Cam Macpherson picked up Blair and me in his open Jeep and we headed to the Pacific coast. The drive through the state of Guerrero was long and hot. Everywhere you looked was nothing but stunted brown cacti.

Finally, as we drove down out of the hills, we saw the Pacific Ocean lying flat and shining like steel. On the outskirts of Acapulco, we turned left on a dirt road that led to our mother's campsite on a beach called the Revolcadero. When we arrived, our mother's body was wet. She had just come out of the water and, without drying off, she showed us around the camp, which consisted of a tent and huts made of palm fronds built, she said, by two Indians in a couple of hours. Blair and I dropped our bags inside of our hut. Here and there you could see chinks of light coming through the walls and roof, but this was Mexico's dry season, so we didn't have to worry about rain. A hose tied over the frond of a palm tree was our shower. Blair and I slept in hammocks. It was hard to sleep because of iguanas rustling in the palm frond roof. I prayed that they would not fall through.

So that we would share her love of Mexico and her feeling of being settled in Cuernavaca, our mother bought us a parrot from a parrot vendor who came knocking at the gate once a week. I spent hours trying in vain to teach the parrot to talk. After about a week I came home from school to find the parrot lying on its back with its

Our mother's camp being built on the
Revolcadero beach, Acapulco, 1950

talons clutched as if it were trying to hold onto a perch. We tried buying smaller parrots, no bigger than my hand, but they died, too. Our mother suspected that the parrot vendor was selling sick parrots. She promised to try to find a parrot in a reputable pet store. Instead of a parrot she came home with two love birds who lived for at least half a year.

Blair and I took riding lessons. Twice a week a *charro*, a professional Mexican rider mounted on a huge black horse and all dressed up with a short, black embroidered jacket and a broad black hat, would ring the bell at the gate. To me, he looked like the essence of Mexico, a powerful man who had to be obeyed. He dismounted and helped us to mount the two horses tethered to his saddle. We rode all over the streets of Cuernavaca. After about half an hour of walking and trotting, the *charro* turned his horse around, came up behind Blair's and my horses, raised his crop, and whipped them hard on the rump. Our horses lurched into a canter. I just leaned forward, clutched the western saddle's horn with both hands, and watched with horror as the pavement rushed by beneath my horse's hooves.

When our mother went to Mexico City to see Edmundo, she often returned with books from the Benjamin Franklin Library. One time she brought home a book about how babies are made, and she insisted on sitting on the terrace and reading it to us. The book had pictures of shapes that I could not imagine being inside of my body, things about which I did not want to know. Blair seemed indifferent. Probably she knew all of this already. I was surprised that our mother did this. She was "doing the right thing," and that was something that she usually didn't bother to do.

Occasionally our mother would take us to Mexico City. She rented one of the flower boats (called *trajineras*) that are paddled like gondolas around the maze of canals in the floating gardens of Xochimilco. Another time, Emundo bought tickets to the water ballet in Chapultepec Park. This was performed at night with dif-

ferent colored lights changing the color of the water in an enormous fountain in and around which the dancers danced. It was the
most glamorous thing I had ever seen. Besides wanting to be a rock
climber when I grew up, I now wanted to join a water ballet troupe.
Or a troupe of flamenco dancers. Our mother bought us rattles and
castanets and hired a flamenco teacher, who soon got pregnant and
stopped coming.

On the weekends, Edmundo was always in a good mood, and
when he smiled his beautiful white teeth shined. He claimed to
be pure Indian, but I could tell by the color of his skin that he
was partly Spanish. Edmundo was generous. He not only paid our
rent, he always brought our mother presents, jewelry mostly, and
sometimes he brought candy for Blair and me. He liked to take us
to expensive restaurants. A few blocks uphill from our house there
was one with peacocks wandering around the garden. After a few
margaritas Edmundo would find everything we said hilarious and
he would laugh so hard he almost cried.

As the months went by, our mother seemed less euphoric about
her life in Cuernavaca. She wasn't painting. I would find her sitting quietly on the veranda staring out into the garden, her eyes
not fixed on any one thing. It was as though her eyes looked backward into her skull instead of out to the flowerbeds and trees. Her
chiseled face (she once told us she had perfect bone structure) was
blank and rigid. Seeing her this way made my heart plunge. She
looked untouchable. I knew that even if I tried to be cheerful and
to make her happy, she would not look at me and smile.

One weekend Edmundo flew into a rage because a gold watch
he had given to our mother was missing. This was the first time I
heard them fight. I do not know why my mother kept picking men
who had bursts of anger. My father never lost his temper—anger
just made him silent. And my mother's own father was as mild as
a teddy bear. Over the next few weeks, I heard raised voices again

and again. Our mother was not a meek person, and her voice be-came increasingly shrill. She didn't care about gold watches, she said. Maybe the parrot vendor or the boy who delivered tortillas stole the watch. Certainly, Chavela could not be blamed. Our maid had had many opportunities to steal things and she never did, so our mother would not let Edmundo question her.

After Christmas, Edmundo stopped coming to Cuernavaca. Our mother had left him because he was a kleptomaniac. He would steal a watch or a piece of jewelry from one woman and give it to another woman. A few years later Edmundo married the daughter of my mother's new husband, Edward Norman. My mother did not approve. Nancy Norman had two children with Edmundo, but he left her and married another wealthy heiress. One day he made his final escape: he moved out of an expensive London hotel and into a cheap one and shot himself.

25

Parque Melchor Ocampo

We're moving to Mexico City," our mother announced. She had found an apartment overlooking Parque Melchor Ocampo, a park that was just a flat piece of hard-packed dirt hemmed in by three streets. The rent was cheap and the location, a few blocks from the Paseo de la Reforma and from Chapultepec Park, was convenient. I was sad to leave our garden and our veranda. Our birds had already died, so my mother promised to get me a dog.

Our new apartment was a modern four-story walk-up. The stairs were made of beige terrazzo, and they smelled of detergent mixed with anti-roach liquid. They were not soft and warm like the terra cotta floors in Cuernavaca. They looked like hotel stairs. The living room where our mother slept had a view of the park. Down a hall were three bedrooms and a kitchen. My bedroom looked out onto another building, and Blair's looked over a side street. After dark Blair and I wrote love letters, folded them into paper airplanes, and, when we saw a man approaching on the street below, we let them fly down to the sidewalk and then watched as the man picked up the letter and read it. Imagine how happy he would be at the thought of being loved.

Our mother took us to register at Greengates, a small English school on Reforma Avenue. Like Miss Heart's, Greengates had forms instead of grades, and the academic level was higher than in American schools. I was far behind in most subjects, but so were the other American children who had recently entered the school.

Algebra was the worst. The Americans in my class had barely learned fractions.

Blair and I walked to and from school on our own. When we reached home, we bought ice cream cones at Chantilly, an ice cream store on the ground floor of our apartment building. In exchange for scoops of ice cream, we gave the two pretty young women behind the counter necklaces that we had strung together out of macaroni we had painted in bright colors. It was a serious transaction. The saleswomen pretended that our necklaces had great value and they made a big to-do about selecting this necklace or that.

Our mother arranged for Blair and me to take ballet lessons. The best thing about ballet class was our new pink cotton ballet costumes whose three-tiered skirts came down just below the bottom of our matching bloomers. I worked hard at all the positions, never being upset by the Russian ballet teacher's harsh commands as she banged out rhythms on the floor with her stick. I snuck glances of myself in the long mirror on the wall to which the ballet bar was attached. My ballet costume made me look thin, and I liked seeing myself as part of a line of girls all in pink and all holding the bar as they did pliés and then pointed their toes out to the side. The pronounced bulge of my calf muscles was something to be proud of.

My mother thought I was a good dancer, but what she really admired were my drawings. She was certain that I would become a painter like herself, and her admiration puffed me up with pleasure. Most of my drawings were of princesses standing between parted curtains. I also made a lot of abstract drawings—just designs in line and color. Those were what my mother liked best. She bought me good-quality paper and a box of pastels. I preferred cheap paper like the newsprint we had used at Dalton. With cheap paper I was not afraid to make a mess.

During this time in Mexico City our mother painted in the living room. She made big still lifes of Mexican fruits, the arrangements of which looked like still lifes by Cézanne. But my mother's brushwork was much wilder. To me, the way her brushstrokes streaked across the canvas showed her own agitation. She also read a lot—books about philosophy, psychology, and Eastern religions. Anything spiritual she loved. It must have been a way of searching for peace. She kept on taking us to the Benjamin Franklin Library, and she also bought us paperbacks from the English bookstore, classics printed on off-white paper that felt rough if you ran your fingers over a page. If you put your nose close to the inside spine, the paper had a wheat-like smell. American books smelled glitzy like new magazines.

At Greengates I met a girl named Johanna Renouf, who became my best friend for the rest of the time that I lived in Mexico. With her long, straight, blonde hair, blue eyes, and pink cheeks, Joanna

Me and Johanna Renouf in the Renouf's
garden, San Ángel, Mexico City, c. 1952

looked like a German girl from the mountains. She lived in the San Ángel section of Mexico City, a district full of grand colonial houses and cobblestone streets. Her father, Edward, was German, an amateur painter and an even more amateur psychoanalyst. He was tall, kindly, and ponderous. Johanna's American mother, Catherine Whittlesey, was quick-witted and elegant in a bohemian sort of way. Johanna had an older sister, Blair's friend Hester, who was really smart but had something of a temper like Susan Howe. Johanna once told me that Hester had said that when I grew up, I was going to have sex appeal. The compliment went into my pool of positive things that I could fish out whenever I felt fat and ugly.

Johanna and I started a show that we called the Hay-Jo Circus. The first thing we did was to go to the pharmacy on San Ángel's central plaza to buy lipstick, rouge, and cold cream with which we planned to remove our makeup after performances. In Johanna's kitchen we invented a kind of cookie—really just an overcooked pancake sprinkled with sugar—to serve as treats for our audience. Edward and Catherine Renouf dutifully exclaimed about how delicious they were. The Renoufs' patio had a swing that we turned into a trapeze upon which we hung upside-down. My circus act was doing cartwheels. Johanna did pirouettes and graceful leaps. Edward and Catherine sat in chairs that we set up and clapped as hard as they could.

Johanna had been at Greengates for several years, so she was not as far behind as I was. She laughed a lot, and when she laughed, she tossed her hair. All the boys loved her. Having Johanna for a friend helped me make other friends. One day at recess six of us snuck into a dark storage room in which four mattresses stood on their sides making two *V*-shaped spaces into which we crawled. It was like being in a huge sandwich. A boy who was my age but smaller than me started caressing my calf. I pretended not to notice. He was a nice boy, and I didn't want to be mean to him, especially because his face was scarred from having been burned. Also, I liked having my leg tickled. When the bell rang for classes, we all rushed out into the light-filled yard. No one looked at anyone else. It was as though nothing had happened.

Soon after we moved into our Mexico City apartment, a new man came into my mother's life, a Spanish refugee who, my mother told me proudly, was Basque and had fought in the Spanish Civil War. Carlos Basurco was smaller than Edmundo, perhaps half an inch taller than my mother. He had black hair combed straight back from his high forehead, sharp features, and small, black eyes that seemed so tightly wound up they might explode. His playing the violin with an orchestra in Bellas Artes (the Palace of Fine Arts) brought prestige but not much money. To support himself he fixed watches. The bedroom next to mine became his watch repair shop. I do not remember any client bringing a watch for Carlos to fix, nor did I ever see him working on a watch. Edmundo had

Carlos Basurco, Mexico City, c. 1951

been more fun than Carlos. Edmundo was ebullient, and his eyes
revealed the feelings that went with what he was saying. Carlos, on
the other hand, had a face like an obsidian mask. Something was
hidden behind the smoky blackness.

My mother thought we needed a dog, and she gave me a two-
month-old Welsh terrier. I named her Chata. My job was to walk
Chata in the park below our building. The park was bleak and
mostly empty. The only playground object was parallel bars that
were too high for me to reach and that were usually occupied by
young men who spent hours pulling themselves up. I steered clear
of them. They were just the types that would tease an American
girl, especially one struggling with a pedigreed dog. Chata was
stubborn. She wouldn't go where I wanted her to go. Sometimes
she made me furious, and I had to stop myself from yanking at her
leash. I didn't want to choke her, so I followed her lead, and in the
end, I usually picked her up and carried her home. At night Chata
slept on one side of me and a stuffed animal slept on the other. I
loved her dog smell and the feeling of her body breathing in and
out against my side.

26

With Family

C hata came with us when Blair and I joined our father and
Mougouch, Maro, Natasha, eight-month-old Antonia, and
a French au pair girl named Mayette at the Turkey Houses in
the beginning of July 1951. When I first arrived at the pond, I
was jealous because Maro and Natasha had been given the turkey
house that I thought of as mine. But I soon got used to the middle cabin. Flanked by two cabins on either side, it felt safe. Also,
Chata could protect me. We spent part of every day at the ocean

Breakfast at the Turkey Houses:
me, Natasha, and Blair, 1951

Andrea Petersen, Blair, Maro, Natasha, Antonia, Mayette
(mother's helper), and me (standing right), 1951

Me doing a cartwheel, 1951

Blair, age fourteen, summer 1951

Me, Maro, Blair, Andrea Petersen,
and Natasha, 1951

dripping wet sand through our fingers to make shapes that looked like spruce trees; building fortresses to keep the tide back; and making cone-shaped, hollow mountains at the bottom of which we lit fires so that the smoke coming out looked like an erupting volcano. In our pond we competed about who could make the most graceful underwater somersault. I still liked to catch things, turtles of course, but also minnows that I could scoop up in cupped hands. Right beside the real pond, I dug out a minnow pond, maybe two feet in diameter. I always ended up digging a channel to the real pond so that the minnows could swim back to their homes.

That September Blair was sent to a girls' boarding school in Northhampton, Massachusetts, a preparatory school for Smith College. Our father and Mougouch decided not to go back to Europe. Instead, they would live with Gaga while they looked for a house to buy in Boston. I was to live with my mother in Mexico City, but for some reason, I do not remember why, soon after I got there, my mother decided that I should not stay. After giving Chata a tranquilizer so that she wouldn't mind being in a crate in the plane's hold, my mother put me on a plane to Boston. When I arrived at Logan Airport and let Chata out of her crate, she was so drugged she couldn't walk. My father was there to meet me, and he was not pleased to see that I had brought my dog.

Gaga came to the door of 63 Garden Street wearing a finely knitted cherry-color dress that showed off her slender frame. She hugged me and then she looked at Chata. "And who is this?" she asked. Mougouch bent down to pat Chata. "Good heavens," she said. "Why didn't your mother let us know? Let's take her into the garden." As soon as I put her down on the grass, the no-longer-sedated Chata raced around as if she were crazy.

That night and every night Chata slept beside me. I did not miss my mother at all. I had learned not to miss the people I was not with. I liked being part of a family. My father seemed glad to have me back, and Mougouch seemed pleased, too. Even though Gaga's house had five big bedrooms on the second floor, all the children lived on the third floor along with Annie and Bessie. We used the back door that gave onto Linnaean Street instead of the grand front entrance, and we used the narrow back stairway instead of the lovely carpeted front staircase with its banister perfect for sliding. I suspect that my father thought that if he kept the children's visibility to a minimum, Gaga would not feel invaded.

Maro, Natasha, and I were enrolled in the Buckingham School where Blair and I had gone when we lived with Gaga two years earlier. The first day of school, we stood with my father on the stoop outside the back door of Gaga's house and waited for the school bus. When the bus pulled up, a chorus of girls' voices shouted out the window, "Look at that handsome Harvard boy!" My father looked up to acknowledge the praise with his charming half smile. Since I had such a good-looking father, I felt sure that I would be able to make friends at Buckingham.

For Thanksgiving we went to my great-aunt Martha's enormous Victorian house in Jamaica Plain, just outside of Boston. All along the length of the dining room table were bowls of walnuts and tangerines. At least twenty-five places had been set. All the guests were relatives—aunts and uncles and cousins, most of whom I hardly knew. Some of Aunt Martha's creepy sons would turn up. Maybe they seemed creepy because of the scandal that ensued when Aunt Martha's husband, Andrew Peters, who briefly served as mayor of Boston, seduced an eleven-year-old girl who was a relative of Aunt Martha's. Maybe they were just born creepy. Blair remembers that once one of them spied on us while we were taking a bath.

Besides Aunt Martha, and of course Gaga, Blair, and my father, the person I loved best at these gatherings was my father's younger brother, Arthur. He had the deepest dimple and a twinkle in his eyes, both of which he must have inherited from Gaga. Uncle Arthur showed me how to crack open a walnut by squeezing two of them together or by placing one nut between my thumb and forefinger and then squeezing hard until the shell split apart. Uncle Arthur really loved his beautiful redhead wife, Betty. With their three children, Marion, John, and Elizabeth (who was born later), Uncle Arthur and Aunt Betty made the perfect family.

All the cousins ate so much that, to make room for pie, we were allowed to run around the table between the turkey course and dessert. After lunch we were sent upstairs to nap, each in our own room. Aunt Martha gave us small note pads with paper in three different pastel shades—pink, blue, and yellow. We could draw on as many sheets of paper as we wanted. We could even take the pads home. After nap time, in order to walk off all the food, our father took us to the Arnold Arboretum, where he told us the names of different kinds of trees and shrubs. I loved that he was knowledgeable, but I didn't pay much attention. Mostly, I just liked being with him.

Every day when we returned home from school, Gaga served tea. Just as she had two years earlier, she wore a velvet floor-length tea gown and she still favored Hu-Kwa tea. To my delight, there on the tea tray were the buttered, thinly sliced white bread and Bessie's cupcakes with white icing. One day I came home from school and Chata was not waiting for me. I looked all over the house and garden. I sat on the back stairs and called and called. No Chata. Instead of Chata, my father came down the stairs. "Chata is not here," he said. "She had distemper and we had to put her to sleep." I said nothing. I pushed past my father, ran upstairs, and flung myself on my bed. I cried so hard—but silently—that I was afraid my throat would fall out. It was as though a part of my body had been ripped off. I remembered how frisky Chata had been that morning. She did not have distemper. I was sure of that. She was just an inconvenience. I never let on that I didn't believe Chata was sick. It might have been Gaga or Mougouch who decided to put Chata down, but I blamed my father. He always ended up doing what the women in his life wanted.

27

Without Blair

In January, I flew back to Mexico City to be with my mother. Being there without Blair was sad. I needed her to give me a picture of the world. My own view of what was happening in our lives depended on the way she saw it. Now our Parque Melchor Ocampo apartment was an immense empty space. Noises sounded like echoes.

My old room was not going to be my room anymore. My mother told me to move my belongings into Blair's room, but I didn't feel like it, so I sat on my bed and rearranged my fuzzy animals. Then I did move my belongings. Blair's room was nicer than mine. Maybe it wasn't so bad. Although I missed Blair, there was a tiny part of me that thought, Now I have my mother all to myself. During the next months, I began to feel that for sure my mother loved me best. She must have known how much I missed Blair because she bought me another dog, this time a fox terrier. I named him Pancho. Carlos was furious. He didn't like small dogs, and he didn't like puppies. Having a dog made me feel I really lived where I lived. I was home. Now I belonged in Mexico and I began to wear my hair in braids that I looped up behind my ears and tied with magenta woolen ribbons. Sometimes, if I was not in a hurry, I wove the ribbons into my braids. This, I was certain, made me look totally Mexican. When Johanna and other Americans living in Mexico talked about the United States, they called it "the States." "I'm going to the States," they would say. Or, "She brought it from the States." It made our country seem far away and not at all important.

With Blair gone, I had to walk to and from Greengates alone. I didn't mind. There was the candy seller on the corner, about a block from school. On a square piece of oilcloth laid on the sidewalk this old woman had rows of round wooden boxes about two inches in diameter and filled with *cajeta*, a caramelized goat's milk. To eat it you used part of the box's top as a scoop. She also sold another kind of candy that tasted like nougat and came wrapped in foil. When you opened the foil, the powdery candy crumbled in your fingers. Each candy's foil wrapping had a different decorative pattern. Every time I ate one, I would smooth out the wrapping and add it to my collection.

After I moved into Blair's bedroom, I tried to make it look as though it had always been mine. Over my bed was a long shelf where Blair had kept books and Kleenex and bracelets that she took off at night. On this shelf I arranged all my stuffed animals and the Toni doll that my mother's sister, Aunt Carolyn, had sent for my birthday. The doll had washable hair and tiny pink curlers. She came wearing a fancy blue dress, so I made skirts and blouses for her out of scraps of fabric. Still, I loved Buttoneyes best. I had had him for such a long time that his brown fur was wearing thin, especially around the metal ring that made his belly play Brahms's lullaby. When I was lonely, I would turn the ring as far as it would go without breaking, and I would press my ear to my bear's belly so that the music felt as if it were inside my head. Even though Buttoneyes was my favorite, I knew that I should not let the other animals feel neglected, so I made a schedule to tell me which animal I should sleep with on which night and Scotch-taped it to the wall beside my bed.

On Sundays, Carlos took my mother and me to bullfights. He was an expert: he had seen a lot of bullfights in Spain, and he told us which matadors we should watch closely. The bullfights opened with a procession of bullfighters walking around the ring to the rhythm of bullfight music. I was enraptured by the men's embroidered jackets and their tight silky pants, and I daydreamed that one day a bullfighter would fall in love with me. Carlos expressed disgust with clumsy picadors. Cowardly matadors sent him into a rage. If a bull was killed with speed and grace, Carlos would roar his approval along with the crowd. The sword was supposed to go down through the back of the bull's neck and straight to the heart. If a bull's death was drawn out, the crowd shouted insults and threw things into the bullring. After a fight, when horses dragged the dead bull away and men came out to sweep new earth over the blood-soaked ground, I was sad.

Once on the way out of the bullring, my mother bought me two pink *banderillas*. These are the spears, each about two feet long and ending in a barb, that picadors plunge into the bull's shoulder to get him mad. Their curly tissue-paper decoration reminded me of the frilly toothpicks that American bartenders stuck into club sandwiches. Although *banderillas* look festive, their tips are sharp and cruel. Like Mexico itself, my mother observed, they mix joy with pain. My mother hung the *banderillas* over the foot of my bed. This gave my room a sophisticated touch: all my mother's artist and writer friends decorated their houses with Mexican craft objects.

Although she was working hard at painting, my mother was an explorer. She was always looking for something new. She had friends she liked to visit who made silver jewelry in Taxco, a mountain town about two hours south of Mexico City. From them she bought a necklace with a big silver cross and earrings that looked like snails. We always visited the clothing shop of Tachi Castillo, where my mother bought me a wraparound circle skirt with an adjustable waistline. It would fit me for a long time, she said. After that, we wandered in the market. To my annoyance, at each stall my mother exclaimed at the beauty of the way the Indian women arranged their fruits, grains, and vegetables on cloths laid over the ground. At one point, she stopped in front of a man selling something fried that he scooped into paper cones. She bought a cone and offered me some. "Fried worms," she said. "They are delicious." I turned away in disgust.

From the market, we would make our way to Los Arcos, a bar from whose balcony we could watch the light change on the cathedral's elaborately carved façade. For lunch, if we were feeling rich or if some wealthy friend invited us, we would drive partway up a mountain to the Hotel Victoria and dine looking down on Taxco and the wide valley below. I watched my mother's face. She saw beauty everywhere. I tried to see it, too, but all I saw was land stretching into the distance.

On one of these trips to Taxco we spent the night with my mother's friend, the writer Eleanor Perenyi. She was brilliant and witty—very certain of her ideas, but she could be unfeeling. Once when her son, Peter, and I were told to go to bed we discovered a scorpion on the wall next to Peter's bed. We ran into the living room to alert the adults. Eleanor said to pay no attention. Brown scorpions were harmless, she insisted. Although the scorpion was gone by the time we returned to our room, neither of us could sleep. All I could think of was the scorpion crawling over my face in the middle of the night.

My mother made sure we went to Taxco for Easter to watch the nighttime ritual of the penitents, the All Souls Procession. From the cathedral on Taxco's main plaza to a church higher up the mountain, men walked barefoot and with their feet chained together. Some of them walked on their knees. They wore black hoods and a black cloth around their loins. Tied to their bare shoulders and outstretched arms were heavy bundles of sticks with thorns that made the men look like Christ carrying his cross. Indeed, they were called *encruzados*. There were also flagellants who carried a cross and whipped their naked backs as they climbed. We stood leaning against the wall of one of the houses that lined the steep cobblestone street. I wished that the street was wider, because the men were so near that the ends of their prickly bundles almost touched my skin. Their backs glistened in the candlelight. Blood trickled through their sweat. Most of the penitents had smooth brown skin and well-muscled shoulders. They were young. I guessed that was why they had sins to be absolved. To my mother, the procession was an aesthetic spectacle. She was enraptured by the slow movement of bodies propelled upward by faith. To her the ritual was filled with elemental poetry. I saw it in more physical terms. The men smelled of sweat. Their knees were raw. Their shoulders were bleeding. Some of them cried out in pain. Some collapsed sideways onto the cobblestones. For me, pity was mixed with revulsion. Suddenly my knees would not hold me up. I knew I was going to faint, even though I had never fainted. In order not to fall, I crouched on the ground. I wanted to vomit. My mother said I must have eaten something bad. I knew I hadn't. The horror of so many men hurting themselves because of faith was overwhelming.

Other weekends we would visit Gustav and Peggy Regler in Tepoztlán, a valley surrounded by rock mountains that rise straight up from the valley floor. The Reglers were the only foreigners living there. To get to their house you had to drive down a hill so steep that I was convinced our car would turn somersaults. After following a rough dirt road for about a mile and a half, we came to a river that surrounded the Reglers' house on three sides. During dry season there was at most an inch of water in it, but during the rainy season the river could be two feet deep. It was touch and go whether we would to get across and up the hill to the Reglers' gate without stalling.

Gustav Regler was a German writer and Communist who served as commissar of the XII International Brigade during the Spanish Civil War and was wounded in the Battle of Guadalajara. He immigrated to Mexico in 1940. In marrying him, Peggy Paul had rebelled against her proper Philadelphia upbringing and became part of Mexico's intellectual bohemia. When he settled in Tepoztlán, Regler, a lover of Goethe, built an octagonal tower for his living room. Goethe, he said, believed that an octagon was the most harmonious space to inhabit. The Reglers' house (which my mother bought in 1953) had a patio with a fountain in the middle. The first time I visited, Gustav took me by the hand and led me to a low stone wall on the far side of the patio and told me that since I was living in Mexico it was important for me to know that under every rock was a scorpion or a tarantula. He then lifted a rock off the wall and out sprang a tarantula—not a huge one, but horribly furry. In all the years I lived in Mexico I never saw another tarantula, but I did see many scorpions, especially after earthquakes when they emerged from their hiding places and scuttled across the floor.

My mother's favorite time to go to Tepoztlán was on the Day of the Dead, when at night everyone visited the graveyard in the fields below the village. Families brought food for their dead and spread out their own meals on the ground. I was embarrassed to be watching this ritual. We were atheists, and they were believers. We were tourists observing the natives, but as in Harlem at Easter, my mother didn't feel out of place. All she cared about was the beauty of the scene. There were candles everywhere. The graves were like little temples painted in bright colors. Children ran about eating pastries in the shape of bones and dangling toy skeletons whose clay bones were connected by springs to make them dance. That morning in the plaza my mother had bought me one and for herself she bought a sugar skull decorated with pink sugar frills that looked like birthday cake icing. The skull had her own name written in pink on its forehead. "It's a way of making fun of death," she explained. "If you laugh at death you can keep it at bay."

The other time that my mother made sure to go to Tepoztlán was during the February carnival when men called *Chinelos* dressed up in velvet tunics, tall conical headdresses, and masks with pointed beards. In the evening they gathered in the village plaza and hopped up and down in a dance called El Brinco (which means "the jump"). As the night wore on, they stumbled from too much tequila. The first time we went to this festival, I danced with two different *Chinelos* and was thrilled to be accepted as if I were Mexican. But a year or two later, the frenzy seemed ready to burst into violence. I could tell that the men were hostile toward gringas. I refused to dance. I felt like sexual prey.

For me the most exciting place to go was to the pyramids of Teotihuacán, which lay about an hour northeast of Mexico City. When we climbed to the top of the Pyramid of the Sun, I felt I was part of something magical, something ancient. What Carlos told me about human sacrifices and blood flowing down the stone steps enhanced the mystery. Climbing back down, my mother and Carlos walked slowly in zigzags to make the descent less steep. I was proud that I could dance my way down.

Carlos Basurco and my mother in the belltower at Acolman,
on the way to Teotihuacán, c. 1951

After a picnic lunch, we walked among the dusty furrows of a nearby field that my mother said was an Aztec graveyard. I had a quick eye for spotting anything that didn't look like earth, so I filled my pockets with pieces of pre-Columbian pottery as well as legs and arms of clay dolls, incense burners, the occasional small stone head, and fragments of faceted obsidian knives.

Carlos liked to go to inexpensive local restaurants where he always ordered steak and fried potatoes. My mother encouraged me to try Mexican dishes such as rabbit stew or roasted goat. If Carlos's steak wasn't served to him medium rare, he would have a temper tantrum. It was embarrassing, especially because he, too, was a foreigner, and his Spanish sounded strange to Mexican ears. Moreover, many Mexicans disliked Spaniards—a hangover from colonial days. The odd thing was that even with this hostility, most Mexicans connected class with skin color, and light skin was prized.

At first, I had liked Carlos, even admired him—he was a musician and also, my mother said, a war hero. But more and more, I came to fear his anger. In one of his bad moods, he nearly kicked Pancho. One day I came home from school and called Pancho in order to take him out. My mother told me that Carlos had taken him for a walk and Pancho had broken free and been run over. I was certain that Carlos had let Pancho off his leash on purpose. He had murdered my dog. I hated him, but I had to hide my hatred to make life easier. My mother depended on Carlos just as she had depended on Edmundo. She had no money of her own except for the $100 that my father was supposed to send once a month for child care. His checks were sporadic, and often we were broke.

Once my mother sent me to buy *pan dulce* at the local bakery. Enveloped by the bakery's warm sugary smell, I piled my tray with pastries. When I took my tray to the cash register it turned out that I didn't have enough money for *pan dulce*. The saleslady

advised me to buy *bolillos* (rolls) instead. Bread was subsidized by
the government in order to make it affordable. Going home with
a package of bread instead of pastry made me see how precarious
life could be. When I was in first grade at Dalton, my mother had
been disdainful about all the rich parents, so being poor carried no
shame. My mother told her friends that Dalton had given Blair and
me scholarships because we were poor artists' children. Now that I
was older, having no money made me anxious. I must have written
to Blair about our finances because she sent a dollar bill in her next
letter. And that dollar actually helped.

My mother did try to earn money. Briefly she taught art at
Greengates. Another moneymaking scheme was to take bolts of
her friend Lena Gordon's hand-woven cloth and sell it in the
United States. We had to drive to the border every six months to
renew our tourist cards, so we could take the cloth with us and mail
it from there. Lena delivered bolts of fabric to our apartment, and
my mother and I sat on the floor and unrolled the cloth. Before
we rolled it back up, my mother brought out baskets full of pre-
Columbian clay figurines. It was not legal to take them out of the
county. If we got stopped at the border, she would pretend that
they were folk art. We wound brightly colored crepe paper around
the figurines to make them look like toys. Then we rolled them
into Lena Gordon's bolts.

The drive to Brownsville took two days. On the American side
of the border we mailed the cloth stuffed with figurines to someone
in New York. Trouble came when we tried to get back into Mexico.
The Mexican officials said there was something wrong with our
tourist cards. They didn't believe that we actually lived in Mexico.
My mother explained that we had been living in Mexico for over a
year. The officials just looked grim, so we went back to the American side and spent the night in a hotel. The following morning, we
bought a bag of peaches and pears and some sandwich materials

for a picnic lunch and headed back to the bridge. At the American side of the border a man in a uniform looked at our papers, took off his glasses, and slowly, slowly wiped them with a tissue. "What," he asked, "is the purpose of your trip?" "Pleasure," said my mother, looking him straight in the eyes. His forehead was sweaty, and a roll of fat bulged over his collar. "Pleasure," he said with a slow fake smile as his eyes went up and down my mother's body. "A Mexican holiday for the little girl, right?" "Yes," my mother said in a voice as icy as Greta Garbo's. "Well, bring me back a piñata," he said as he stamped our papers. My mother smiled her most superior smile. "Thank you," she said. As we moved toward the door, he reached out to pat my head, but I ducked just in time and moved to the other side of my mother.

At the Mexican customs office, my mother once again told the officials that we lived in Mexico. They relented only after my mother showed them my diary, which proved that I went to school in Mexico City. We had driven only a few miles into Mexico when I realized that I had left my Brownie camera in the hotel room. My mother just turned the car around and headed back to the United States. The customs officer on the American side of the bridge peered into the Coche de Mama. "You can't take that fruit into the United States," he announced, pointing to my half-eaten peach. "But it's American fruit," my mother protested. "We just bought it on the American side." "I don't make the rules, ma'am." "All right," said my mother. "We'll eat it here." We sat on the Coche de Mama's fender and ate the entire bag of fruit. She offered the customs officer a peach. He said it was against the law for him to accept it, so he just stood there and watched us eat. I was embarrassed, but my mother didn't mind at all.

Soon after our return to Mexico City, my mother announced that she and I were going to visit Lena Gordon in Erongarícuaro, a village on Lake Pátzcuaro in the state of Michoacán. The timing of our visit had to do with a particular fiesta, a day on which at a certain moment all the village craftsmen and shopkeepers throw samples of what they make or sell into the air and children, even adults, scramble to pick them up.

In the late afternoon, Lena led us to the central plaza to watch the tossing up of craft objects. She carried a basket full of carefully wrapped samples of her cloth, which she planned to fling into the air. Dark clouds were amassing to the north, and we could hear distant thunder. All of a sudden it began to rain so hard that the water came down from roofs in sheets. We took shelter in a portico on one side of the plaza. "They are going to have the fiesta in spite of the rain," Lena said. A band set up in an ornate covered bandstand played loud music, and there were a few halfhearted fireworks. When a horn blew, the gifts were thrown up into the rain-filled air. People ran to collect what they could.

Except for a few people under the portico and the musicians who were packing up to go home, the plaza was soon empty. But then I saw a little girl, maybe eight years old, running across one corner of the plaza. She must have seen some bundle that no one had taken. There was a flash of lightning and she fell. People rushed to help. When they picked her up, her body was limp. Lena went over and took her pulse. The girl was unconscious but alive. Because Lena was the only foreigner living in this village, she had some authority. She asked the girl's parents to let her drive their daughter to the nearest town that had a doctor. They refused. Instead, they carried the girl home. We followed at a distance. The girl's family laid her on a metal cart outside of their house. Lena kept telling them that their daughter should be inside and wrapped up in blankets. A little brandy would help. No one listened. Lena lost her temper. The girl's rain-soaked dress stuck to her body. On the surface of the cart where she lay there were pieces of broken glass. Raindrops bounced off the glass shards, then pooled around them. Lena drove off to find a doctor in a nearby town but returned without one. The doctor had been summoned to another village.

By this time, the girl's family had brought her inside and laid her out on a sheet spread on the floor. At each corner of the sheet a candle burned. Her family thought they were sending her to heaven with their prayers. The girl still had a pulse, Lena said, but they were treating her as if she were dead. Now Lena kept her rage in check. It is not for a foreigner to oppose the rituals of her adopted home. Back at Lena's house, my mother and Lena poured themselves tequila with no ice. I watched the storm clouds pass over the lake. Pátzcuaro's fishing boats with their butterfly nets were not out. The water looked gray. The sight of the dying girl did not leave my eyes. It was as though a tiny image of her dying body was stuck under my eyelids. I had always believed in the efficacy of willpower. Now I saw that sometimes even a powerful adult cannot change the course of events.

28

Escuela Pan Americana

At first the girls in my form at Greengates School had crushes on our handsome young math teacher. His English accent was a big attraction. But what he was teaching was incomprehensible. One day when an American girl named Toy Bauman was whispering in my ear, the math teacher walked slowly over to her desk and slammed the spine of a book onto the side of her head. Johanna and I were shocked. We didn't think that teachers had the right to hit a child. At recess Johanna, Toy, and I huddled near the school's gate. We decided to walk out of Greengates and never return. On the sidewalk outside the gate we laughed and joked to keep up our courage. What if our parents made us go back to Greengates? Then we would be in real trouble. When I got home and told my mother what happened, she telephoned Catherine Renouf, and together they decided to send Johanna and me to the Pan American School.

I had to take two different buses to get there. That was okay most of the time. From the bus window, I saw fancy apartment buildings and rundown houses, and I thought about the multitude of people living behind those windows. Like me, each person thought their home was the center of the world. I liked the anonymity of riding on a bus. I could pretend I was just a Mexican girl on her way to school. And buses were fun: passengers chatted as though they knew one another. Many Mexican voices talking at once makes a gentle warble, quite unlike the grating sound of New

York City bus riders. Some passengers carried enormous bundles, even bunches of live chickens tied by their ankles. Mothers with their babies wrapped in *rebozos* seemed so calm, so accepting of the life fate had dealt them.

One bad thing about riding a bus was sitting next to a beggar. I was afraid of catching leprosy. Once a ragged and filthy man sat down next to me. Soon his shoulder and thigh were intruding in my space. I glared at him, but he looked straight ahead. Every time I moved closer to the window, he moved closer to me. I was about to change seats when I noticed that his fly was open and his penis, which looked diseased, lay on his lap. I pretended I didn't see it. I couldn't change seats because I would have had to pass in front of his knees and his penis was right there. Should I feel sorry for him, I wondered. Could his penis be out because the cloth of his trousers chafed? I just held my breath and looked out the window until, at last, he stood up, turned to look at me, and got off the bus. Even with him gone I felt sullied.

Every morning when I arrived at the Pan American School, the first thing that happened was the entire student body lined up in straight rows in the school's large yard. A loudspeaker played martial music, and a man's voice made announcements. For about ten minutes we marched in formation around the yard. Then we saluted the Mexican flag and sang the Mexican national anthem. I liked being part of a big group, but I didn't know anyone except Johanna, who, because she was fluent in Spanish, was put in the Spanish-language section and a grade ahead of me.

Blair came for spring vacation. My mother and I went to pick her up at the airport, and when Blair cleared customs and came toward us, I saw my mother's face tighten. Her eyes seemed to bore into Blair's face and body. I hoped that Blair did not see that look of scorn. It was a look that made you feel ugly. Recently she had not given me that look because, even though I was fat, she was convinced that I was artistic. She gave Blair a kiss on the cheek. Her kisses always felt hard because of her prominent cheekbones. When we got into the Coche de Mama, she turned to Blair and said she thought Blair's new permanent wave looked common. Worse still, Blair was wearing red lipstick and nail polish. She had lost a lot of weight, and her breasts had grown. Her long legs curved in and out at the right places, and her face looked even more like a Greek goddess than it had a few months ago. The problem was that now that Blair looked almost like a woman, men turned their heads and stared. Our mother was used to being the only attraction.

Blair's vacation did not go well. She was angry with our mother, and she thought I was babyish. I had always worshiped Blair. Most of the time she had not minded if I followed her around, and sometimes we played together as if we were the same age. Now I secretly agreed with our mother that Blair's taste had been corrupted by her boarding-school friends. Thinking this made me feel guilty. I should have protected Blair from our mother's meanness.

Toward the end of spring, Lena Gordon told my mother that her daughter, Margarita, was going to stop going to school in order

Me and Blair, Cuernavaca, 1952

to dedicate herself to dance. Margarita was a year older than me, thin, exotic-looking with dark eyes and skin. She looked completely Mayan, my mother said. I was fascinated by Margarita's outspoken, flamboyant, and willful behavior. She made us laugh. She didn't care what people thought. We had both given up ballet and were now studying modern dance with a woman named Waldeen (her real name was Waldeen Falkenstein) whose choreography was full of intense and primitivistic gestures that connected more with the earth than with the sky. I was almost as good a dancer as Margarita, so my mother decided that I, too, should give up going to school and just work toward becoming a dancer. I refused to leave school. I thought that my mother's wanting me to leave school came from her narcissism. She just wanted to show what a free spirit she was. It would be something amusing to talk about.

In June 1952, my mother put me on a plane. I was to stay at Aunt Carolyn's in New York for a few days and then take a train to Boston, where my father would pick me up and take me to Cape Cod. Standing in line to give my ticket to an official at the Mexico City airport, I felt almost like an adult. As I climbed the steps and into the Pan American plane, I tried to look nonchalant, as though I traveled alone all the time. The flight was not nonstop. I was supposed to change planes in some Texan city and continue on to New York. When I presented my ticket for the second leg of the trip, the Texan agent said that what I had handed him was a receipt, not a valid ticket. I dug around in my purse. There was no ticket there. What had happened was that the ticket agent in Mexico had taken the tickets for both flights. The Texan agent would not allow me to board the plane. I felt lost, afraid that I would be stuck in this airport forever and would never reach home. I cried and cried, but the man still would not let me on the plane. There was a line of passengers behind me waiting to present their tickets. An American woman came up to me, and when I explained about the lost ticket, she bought me another one. She sat beside me on the plane, and when we landed in New York she took me to Aunt Carolyn's apartment, and Aunt Carolyn reimbursed her for my ticket. I was glad to be safe, but I also felt embarrassed that the woman had had to buy me a ticket and bring me into the city. Aunt Carolyn was furious at my mother for choosing a flight that required changing planes. My aunt disapproved of my mother anyway. She didn't like the way my mother kept changing men, and she thought that my mother ought to have a job and help support Granny and Granddaddy.

A day or so later, Aunt Carolyn took me to Grand Central and put me on a train to Boston, where my father was waiting for me. It was already dark when we reached the dirt road that leads from Route 6 to Horseleech Pond. I was lying on the backseat, half asleep. My father was a good driver, but he went fast over bumps. If I opened my eyes and saw trees speeding by, I was sure we were going to crash into one of them. Every time we climbed a hill, I was afraid that when we reached the top, the car would keep on going up and we would be lost in the sky forever.

Except for the fact that Mougouch and my father had a new baby, Susannah, born in April, the days on Horseleech Pond followed their familiar pattern—walking on sand, walking on pine needles, fresh water, saltwater, avoiding lily pads, and, at the ocean, diving through waves or doing belly flops over them. At low tide I liked to stand in shallow water at one end of a sand flat and then step into the *V* where small waves coming from different directions converged and bubbled up around my ankles. Standing in this vortex was like being in the middle of the universe.

The only bad thing that summer was that Mougouch was exhausted from having two babies (Antonia was only one and a half) as well as four other girls to look after. Little things bothered her. She got furious, for example, when she found what she thought was my mother's lipstick under her bureau. I didn't tell her, but

My father, Natasha, Mike (Blair's boarding school room-
mate), and Maro in front of a turkey house porch, 1952

that lipstick had belonged to my father's third wife, Dasya, not to
my mother.

One night we had a bonfire on the shore of the pond. Mougouch told us girls to observe it carefully, because afterward we
were going to draw our impressions of the fire and there would
be a prize for the best drawing. She gave us a big box of colored pencils and drawing pads with beige cloth covers and beige
cotton ties to keep them closed. These notebooks had once belonged to her dead husband, the painter Arshile Gorky, and there
were a few of his drawings on the first pages of mine. I drew an
orange and yellow fire rising from red coals and surrounded by
a black sky. To my surprise, my drawing won the prize—a box of
sugar doughnuts. Mougouch must have chosen my drawing instead of Maro's to be nice. She was always extra nice to me, even
better than a mother. I tried to be extra nice back. I did things

like clearing the table or holding Antonia to earn Mougouch's approval.

In August Blair and I took a train to Bath, Maine. Gaga picked us up at the station and drove us to her house high above the ocean in Small Point. Life here was much less formal than it had been at 63 Garden Street. Screen doors slammed, lunch was like a picnic on the porch. Since I didn't have many summer clothes, Gaga took me into Bath and bought me a Lanz of Slazburg jumper. It was pink with two rows of rickrack above the hem and small pearl buttons down the front. It was the best dress I had ever owned. As she had when we lived with her in Cambridge, Gaga played the piano while Blair and I danced. We wore the matching ballet costumes from our Mexico City ballet school. Blair looked glamorous in hers. I just looked chubby and cute.

Near Gaga's house was a steep path that wound through a thicket of small pines and down to a beach that was hemmed in on either side by rock cliffs. The sand was darker than our Truro beach

Blair and me (in Mexican ballet costumes) with Gaga's dog,
Echo, on Gaga's porch in Smallpoint, ME, 1952

sand and full of pebbles and small shells. Once, at low tide Blair and I walked around the cliff on the right side of the beach and followed a little path going up through some woods. We wanted to see where the path led. Suddenly Blair remembered that Gaga had warned us not to go around the cliff. By the time we had climbed back down to the shore, the tide had come in and waves were breaking against the outer edge of the rock promontory. I didn't think we would be able to get around and back to Gaga's beach, but Blair said we had to. "Wait until the next wave pulls back," she said. "Then we'll make a run for it while the water is shallow." "Now!" she shouted, and we ran through the receding wave and made it around the rock just as the next wave came crashing down.

29

Betrayal

B ack in Mexico City that fall, living with Carlos Basurco became increasingly tense. Once he got into such a rage at our
maid that he pushed her down the stairs. At night I could hear
shouting at the other end of the apartment. One Saturday morning my mother came into my room with a small canvas bag. "Pack
up your nightgown, toothbrush, and your hairbrush. You'll also
need a change of clothes." She looked scared, which was unusual
for her. "We have to leave right now." I grabbed Buttoneyes. "Can
I take him?" She said I could, so I squished him into the top of
my bag. Even with the living room door closed, I could hear the
squawks and screeches of Carlos's bow moving over his violin. We
did not say good-bye to him, we just snuck out the door and raced
down the stairs. The Coche de Mama was parked right outside. We
jumped in and drove to San Ángel. My mother explained that she
was leaving Carlos and that I was to stay at the Renoufs' until she
could figure out what to do next.

At the Renoufs' I slept in Edward Renouf's soundproof office
where he occasionally saw patients for psychoanalysis. The room
was close to the front door, so at night I had to force myself not
to listen for intruders. One morning when I was making my bed,
I found a scorpion tucked into the end of the mattress. Edward
Renouf removed it with a pair of tongs. Even after he killed it, the
scorpion's tail rose up to strike. I pretended that I was used to scorpions. I was a guest. I should not make trouble.

I had been living with the Renoufs for a week when my mother came to pick me up. I stuffed my belongings into my bag, said good-bye to the Renoufs, and went out to the Coche de Mama. I almost didn't get in. Carlos was in the driver's seat. As we headed north along Insurgentes Avenue, no one spoke. Finally, Carlos turned his head and fixed his obsidian eyes on me. "I hear you are afraid of me," he said in a mocking voice. Now I hated Carlos even more than I had before and I hated my mother, too. She had betrayed me. She should not have told Carlos what I had said. It meant she cared more about him than about me. In the days that followed, I refused to speak to Carlos, and I answered my mother with monosyllables. Luckily, my life at Parque Melchor Ocampo didn't last much longer. A week or so later, my mother told me she was leaving Carlos for good and that I was going to spend the rest of the school year with my father, who had bought a whole house on Myrtle Street on Boston's Beacon Hill. There was lots of room for me.

This time my mother and I flew to New York together. We stayed with Aunt Carolyn while we visited Granny. The walls in Granny's apartment were even browner than they had been in 1948 when we left New York. Although she had been treated several times with electric shock, her cycle of depression and mania continued. When she was manic, she talked on the telephone nonstop. My mother would hold the receiver far from her ear or she would put the phone down and leave the room. In her manic phases, Granny would go to Bloomingdale's and shop as if she were a millionaire. Aunt Carolyn had to return everything she bought. When depressed, Granny would grab my hand and ask, "Is everything all right?" I forced myself not to pull my hand away. "Everything is okay," I told her in the most soothing voice I could muster.

Aunt Carolyn was my mother's opposite. She was good-looking

but not quite beautiful. When they were girls, my grandfather was seduced by his oldest daughter's beauty. It was obvious that my mother was his favorite. She remembered being allowed to read at the table even though her parents knew it was bad manners. Aunt Carolyn was not given this privilege. She was less fascinating, less of a rebel force. My mother was given permission to leave the Chapin School early each day in order to study painting at

My mother and Aunt Carolyn ice skating in
Central Park, c. 1920

Aunt Carolyn and her son, Jim Sheffield,
with Blair and my mother in Central Park, 1938

the Art Students League. She longed for freedom and sometimes she took it. With a friend, she made a plan to climb onto Chapin's roof to meet some boys from a school next door. Her friend got scared and backed out, so my mother went to the roof alone. She was caught. When she was brought before the student council, its president, Anne Morrow (later Lindbergh) said she would pray for my mother.

Aunt Carolyn moved in high social circles. She was married to a prominent lawyer named Frederick Sheffield. Their friends were people like Herbert Brownell (Eisenhower's attorney general), Laurance Rockefeller, and John Lindsay, who, after graduating from Yale law school in 1948, joined my uncle Freddy's law firm and later served as New York's mayor. Aunt Carolyn's Fifth Avenue apartment was furnished with proper upper-class furniture—lots of mahogany. She always wore subdued, expensive, non-body-revealing clothes, and she belonged to a fashionable women's club. My cousins went to the best schools. Even though Aunt Carolyn's youngest daughter Ann was a year younger than me, I was in awe of her. She must have been really smart to do so well at the Brearley School. I didn't think I could ever get into that school. Even though I did not want Aunt Carolyn to be my mother, I wished my mother were more like her. After a couple of days, my mother could no longer tolerate Aunt Carolyn's critical gaze. Before taking off to visit an artist friend in Springs on Long Island, she put me on a train for Boston, where my father picked me up and took me to his new house at 83 Myrtle Street.

30

Myrtle Street

The Myrtle Street house was at the top of Beacon Hill not far from the State House. This area, called "the back side of the hill," was considered to be a slum even though it was only a few blocks from the hill's fashionable section. Most of the narrow brown houses with stoops were occupied by Italian families. Their children played on the street, but Maro and Natasha and I never played with them. They already had their cliques and hangouts. We were new people. They didn't need us.

When I arrived in Boston, Maro and Natasha had already started at the Brimmer and May School. Mougouch charmed the headmistress, and I was allowed to join the seventh grade immediately. The teachers were good, especially the art teacher. Team sports were a problem. I was outfitted with a dark blue gym costume complete with navy bloomers. They gave me shin guards and a hockey stick, and a bus took the hockey players to a field outside of the city. I also learned to dribble a basketball across the school's gymnasium and how to shoot baskets. At both games I was the worst player in my class, so I just tried to keep out of my teammates' way.

By January I had made a friend, Pattie Sullivan, who was the only other fat girl in my class. Pattie seemed not to mind being fat. She felt popular anyway, and she was—perhaps being rich and clever gave her extra confidence. She always wore a plaid pleated skirt and a dark blue wool Scotch cap with a band of plaid trim.

Her white blouses were perfectly ironed. Most days she and I walked home from Brimmer and May together. We crossed Chestnut Street and started the climb up Beacon Hill to Pattie's red brick house on Louisburg Square, one of the fanciest places on the Hill. As I continued on alone up to Myrtle Street, the streets got darker, the houses looked squeezed together and were less well kept.

Mougouch treated me like another daughter, just as my father treated Maro and Natasha as if they were his own children. That they called him Daddy no longer bothered me. By now I thought of them as real sisters. For a time, they even adopted Phillips as their last name. To ward off the winter cold, Mougouch had a navy-blue woolen cape (a copy of a French policeman's cape) made for me. Maro and Natasha already had identical capes. I was grateful to be included. When we walked to school, we felt like triplets.

For Gaga's sake and for the sake of Mougouch's mother, Essie Magruder, Antonia and Susannah were going to be christened at Trinity Church. I asked if I could be christened, too. I wanted to be christened because I wanted Mougouch to be my mother. For godmothers I chose her and Anna Matson. My father chose Fuller Potter to be my godfather. Mougouch took me to the Chubbettes department at Filene's to buy a new dress for the christening. It was turquoise, too bright a color for a christening, I thought, but it was the only dress that fit. Maro, Natasha, and I started going to Sunday school. I listened attentively to Bible stories, and I treasured the pictures of Jesus and Mary and saints that they gave us to take home. Learning about Christianity was for me a little like learning about birds: just as I had memorized the images in the bird book Gaga gave me, now I stored Bible pictures in my head.

Gaga and Essie came to the christening. During the ceremony, which, since there were three of us, took quite a while, Mougouch had an amused smile. My father looked serious. Even though he was not at all religious, he was solemn in churches. I was solemn, too. I figured that being christened was a way of attaching myself to God and of making him love me if he really did exist up there. For a christening present, Essie gave me a Bible with very thin crinkly paper, a black leather cover, and a ribbon to mark your place. After being baptized I became devout. I put a stool next to my bed and on it I placed a candle and my Bible. Before going to sleep at night I read a few pages, sometimes the Old Testament, sometimes the New. This phase only lasted a few months. By the time I got to Horseleech Pond in June, I had forgotten about God.

Until a French au pair girl named Almut arrived to help with the cooking and cleaning, Mougouch had had to clean the house by herself, and it had four floors with a steep, narrow, carpeted staircase. When she vacuumed the stairs, Mougouch wore a red cotton bandana to keep her hair out of her eyes. It made her face look red with anger. We learned to keep away from her when she was wielding the vacuum. At Myrtle Street I did everything I could to make Mougouch like me. I didn't want to be a burden. If I was agreeable and a good influence on my younger sisters, she would be glad to keep me around.

Maro was two and a half years younger than me, but she acted the same age. She was funny, mischievous, and not at all shy. She was my best friend. No matter who was in the room, Maro always had to be the most powerful and dramatic person present. Her background was much more interesting than Blair's and mine, she said. We were just boring New Englanders, whereas her father was Russian from the Caucasus. Or maybe he was Armenian; she wasn't sure. My father was just a talented printmaker who sometimes painted. Her father was a famous painter.

Arshile Gorky's paintings hung in the living room of our Myrtle Street house, and Mougouch did her best to keep the art world aware of Gorky's importance. I hoped that my father didn't mind being married to a woman who believed so passionately in her first husband's genius. Maro and I used to look at her father's paintings and try to figure out what his forms meant. In one canvas we saw a rabbit with perfectly depicted rabbit ears. Bugs Bunny we called him. Gorky's curving, swooping lines and his visceral shapes made me wonder why on earth he had painted them the way he did.

Maro used to take out all of her dead father's art books and study them as she lay on her stomach on the living room carpet. Often, I joined her. The book that I liked best was about Toulouse-Lautrec. It was a view into such a different world—women doing the can-can in a music hall or drinking absinthe alone at a café table. Maro was convinced that she drew so well because she had inherited Gorky's genius. But when Brimmer and May had a contest and all the girls were asked to make a poster for a lecture that the cartoonist Al Capp (who created the comic strip *Li'l Abner*) was going to give at the school, Al Capp chose my poster as the best of all. The prize was *Fifty Centuries of Art*, a book about the history of art for young people published by the Metropolitan Museum of Art. Memorizing the paintings in this book was even more fun than memorizing birds in my bird book or the holy images I took home from Sunday School.

We loved Natasha, but Maro and I teased her by running away from her, racing from the front hall to the kitchen, through a swinging door into the dining room, and then back into the front hall. Since all three of us were laughing, it didn't seem mean. Natasha lived a fantasy life inside her six-year-old head. We often called her "poor Natasha." Even my father teased Natasha. She spent a lot of time cutting up paper to make little things, and when he passed the door of her bedroom, he would say, "Little tiny pieces of paper!"

That winter, Mougouch became increasingly restive. It was dark at 3:30 and she had too many children to look after. Social life in Boston did not interest her. Most of her good friends were in the art world, and they lived in New York. She and my father did go out to lectures and other cultural events, and when they did, I loved watching Mougouch get ready. Her dressing table had a large oval mirror with posts on either side to hold it up. She used the posts to hang her many necklaces—necklaces with chunky beads, some with American Indian silver beads and turquoises, others with small bones that must have been animals' teeth. Mougouch smelled wonderful when she kissed us good night. Her dressing table had several perfume bottles—among them, Joy and Vent Vert. When Mougouch said good night, she wasn't in a rush, and she would accompany the kiss with a little hug. My mother's kisses were brisk, as if kissing were simply a duty to be performed before she went out. Mougouch was thirteen years younger than my mother. When she walked, there was a spring in her step.

Nineteen fifty-three—another Cape Cod summer with the usual activities: beach picnics, blueberry picking, riding ocean waves. Blair was sixteen, so she could go out at night with boys. Once when my father and Mougouch and Blair were out, Maro, Natasha, and I were allowed to sleep together on sofas in the main

Penny Jencks and her horse, Bobby, with
Andrea, Maro, and Natasha, 1952

house rather than in our Turkey Houses. Blair came home from a date with Peter Chermayeff and told us that Peter had kissed her, but she didn't really like it. (Another time she told us that he was a wonderful kisser.) She said that Peter had told her that he was going to marry Maro, Natasha, or Andrea Petersen, a pretty girl Maro's age who lived right next door to Peter in one of our father's army barracks houses on Slough Pond. None of my sisters knew about my crush on Peter. That night I cried into my pillow, but not loud enough for anyone to hear.

31

Edward Norman

Halfway through the summer, my mother called and said she wanted Blair and me to come and live with her in Provincetown. I did not want to leave Horseleech Pond. I think I loved the pond more than I loved my mother and father. The pond I could trust. It wasn't going to leave me. When I was in the pond, every part of my body was held. Also, life with my father and Mougouch seemed more normal to me than life with my mother. I liked being one of a bunch of girls. My mother lived as if she were running at the edge of an abyss. Some of her adventures were exciting; others seemed destined to blast everything apart. I didn't want to live in smithereens. I told my father that when he and Mougouch went to Italy at the end of the summer, I wanted to go with him. He said he would tell my mother that this was what I wanted. It was, he assured me, what he wanted, too.

There was no getting out of going to live with my mother. She had rented two houses overlooking the bay in the west end of Provincetown. On the second floor the houses were joined by a bridge. The reason my mother could afford these houses was that she had a new lover and he was rich. When my father dropped Blair and me at my mother's house, she came out and gave him a hug. I watched them closely to see if he had already told her about my wanting to go and live with him in Europe. My mother was relaxed, so I guessed that my father had not said anything yet. She showed Blair and me our new bedrooms on the first floor. Her own bedroom took up the whole top floor. Half of it she used as a studio. To get to it, you had to climb stairs that were more like a ladder and then raise a trap door. I was glad she was on another floor because I felt like being alone. In a few months I would turn thirteen, and I was moody. I missed Horseleech Pond. I spent a lot of time in my room.

At what my mother always called "the legal drinking hour" (six o'clock), Edward Norman, her new man, came over from his house—the one next door connected to ours by a bridge. He was nice looking, slightly bald, and he had a soft, smooth voice. His manner was more formal than that of her other men. His clothes were more formal, too. He wore good-quality cotton slacks and Brooks Brothers–style shirts. Most of my mother's artist friends dressed in old faded clothes. They didn't have to go to offices. Also, they didn't want to look rich. Edward gave Blair and me each a box of chocolates. He must have been trying to make us like him.

During the first days in Provincetown, our mother took us along when she went to see friends like Roger Rilleau in his leather-working studio on Commercial Street. For Provincetown's bohemians, Roger made Greek-style sandals with soles shaped to

Edward Norman, c. 1954

Edward Norman and my mother, c. 1954

fit the wearer's arch. My mother ordered a pair of sandals, and since they required several fittings, we went to Rilleau's workshop often. I could see that my mother enjoyed having the handsome Roger touch her feet as he adjusted her sandals' fit.

We spent a lot of time at Herman and Sunny Tasha's hilltop house on Provincetown's East End. I knew them from other summers when Herman took our mother, Blair, and me out on his fishing boat for the Blessing of the Fleet. On Herman's boat there was a lot of drinking. It didn't matter: Sunny always made trays of brownies, and I ignored the rising hilarity of the adults' tipsy voices. The only annoying thing was that my mother sat in the prow leaning back on her elbows as if she were relishing the sun and the breeze running through her hair. I thought she was posing for Herman Tasha's benefit. She was what she called a "great beauty," and she was flaunting it. My mother was wearing shorts and a wide leather belt, a low-cut shirt, and a huge Mexican silver cross that hung from a silver choker. The cross made me mad, too. My mother was against religion—she had been furious when I got christened. Even though she loved cathedrals, she disliked Catholicism, which in Mexico, she said, kept the *campesinos* ignorant and poor. I could tell that she wore the cross because it made her look poetic.

Whenever I visited the Tasha's ramshackle home, I entered through the back door, which led directly into the kitchen. Sunny would be at the stove flipping tinker mackerel. Although I didn't like fish, I liked the crispy fish that Sunny cooked. I would make my way through several dark interior rooms and come out on the back porch where I would find my summertime best friend, Carla Tasha curled up on a beat-up swinging love seat. In the yard beneath a shade tree, a car tire hung from a rope. Carla and I took turns swinging on it. The Tashas' goats and chickens would gather around, nosing and scratching about for something to eat.

Our mother signed Blair and me up for sailing and ballet lessons. Other than dance classes, my mother had never bothered with lessons before, not even swimming lessons. Tennis and golf lessons were bourgeois, she thought. We spent most of the ballet classes preparing for a performance of *The Nutcracker*. Blair had a really good part—she was a seductive Arabian dancer wearing silk pantaloons and not much on top. I was a Russian dancer, a plump peasant galumphing around the stage.

32

Beach Glass

We had been living with our mother for a little over a week when she told me that my father had called and said that he wanted me to live with him in Florence. My mother said she would not allow this. She and my father were going to go to court to fight for custody of me. The court was in Barnstable, a big town about an hour away. I would have to appear before the judge and say which parent I wanted to live with. When she told me that I could not go to Italy, my mother seemed angry. Perhaps she was simply hurt. I had never seen her with hurt feelings, so I guessed it must be anger. She didn't raise her voice, but her words had a glint, like steel. Her features looked as sharp as an Apache. Maybe it was true that she had Native American blood. I said I wanted to live with my father and that I didn't want to go back to Mexico. I didn't tell her, but I was tired of her succession of men. She refused to listen. I was sure she only wanted me with her because of her vanity. To have a daughter who did not want to live with her must have been humiliating.

I stomped into my room and closed the door. I was so mad I couldn't even cry, so I escaped from the house by a side door and went for a high-tide swim. Water always collected the pieces of me and put them back together. The bay was calm and clear with hardly any seaweed, but I liked our pond water better. At dinner that evening I refused to speak. I didn't even look at Edward Norman. Blair talked and talked about a dancing party that she planned to give a few weeks hence. She didn't notice that there was any tension.

The next morning seagulls woke me early. They find clams on the sand flats, fly high up, and drop them on the rocks to break open their shells. Then they squabble about which gull gets to eat the clam. There is something melancholy about seagulls' cries. They go on and on regardless of whether I hear them, and they will keep crying that same cry even after I am dead.

With the tide out, the beach was hard and wide. Except for the tracks of seagulls, the first footprints were mine. When I walked under the old wharfs near our house, the air was cool and had a pungent smell that came from the bright-green ruffles of seaweed attached to the posts. To make my footprints disappear, I walked in the water for a little while. My mother would never find me. This beach had a lot of frosted sea glass. Every few feet I found another piece. Blue was the best, but hard to find. Maybe only broken Milk of Magnesia bottles made blue glass. Red glass was rare, too. There was a lot of brown and green and quite a bit of my favorites, a pale turquoise and a pinky lavender. I filled my pockets with the most interesting shapes. When I got home, I laid them out on my bureau. They were like little abstract sculptures.

Later that day I walked two blocks east on Commercial Street to Dyer's hardware store and bought copper wire. Back in my bedroom, I made a choker out of twisted wire and then wound copper wire around pieces of beach glass, crossing and recrossing the wire to create a strong design. I gave each piece of glass a three-inch length of wire so that I could attach it to the choker. Once I had enough necklaces, I set up a card table on the sidewalk. Passersby stopped. Some of them bought. My necklaces cost $1.50. I also made mobiles and a few collages out of beach glass. Nobody bought those. Occasionally I took necklaces and some clamshells that I had painted with seascapes and sold them on MacMillan

Wharf. I timed it so that I would be ready when the Boston boat pulled in and hundreds of tourists poured down the wharf and into town. Some of them threw dimes into the bay so that local boys could dive for them. When one of them saw my wares, she cried, "Oh, look at that cute little Portuguese girl!" I was delighted to be taken for a fisherman's daughter.

My mother's friends—especially her artist friends—loved my necklaces. One buyer was a rich lady who lived in one of my father's beach houses. She ordered a necklace with green and brown glass to go with her brown eyes and dark brown hair. When I delivered it to her, she didn't have the $1.50 to pay for it. She said she would pay me next time. She never paid, and I never forgot her debt. I liked making money. With money of my own I was safe. By the end of the summer I had made over one hundred and fifty dollars, which I deposited at the Seamen's Savings Bank. I was so proud when Provincetown's *Advocate* ran an article about me and my necklaces and how much I had earned.

This was the first summer that I cared about getting a suntan. Edward bought Blair and me good-quality blue-and-red canvas air mattresses upon which we floated to get the backs of our legs brown. One day there must have been an unusual current and we suddenly found ourselves halfway across the bay. The sky beyond Long Point was turning dark. There was distant thunder. Paddling as fast as we could, we made it home just before the rain. Our mother had not even noticed we'd been gone. It was unfair: she gave us complete freedom, but she still wouldn't let me go and live with my father.

After a few weeks in Provincetown, I realized that the little bridge between my mother's bedroom and Edward Norman's bedroom in the house next door had a purpose. One morning I needed to ask my mother something and I climbed the ladder and pushed open the trap door. There was Edward naked and just about to climb on top of my naked mother. She screamed, and I closed the trap door and backed down the ladder. My heart pounding, I went into my room, shut the door, and tried to erase what I had seen from my mind. Neither my mother nor Edward ever mentioned the episode. I can still see my mother's horrified face when she saw me.

Being naked usually did not bother my mother. She loved her body and was happy to show it off. But for her, nudity was not an invitation. She was an aesthetic object. That summer, she hung a photograph of her naked breast with a cluster of wet grapes on top of it on the living room wall. I knew this photograph was meant to be artistic, but I didn't want Blair's and my friends to see her breast swelling like a sand dune and covered with goose bumps—the grapes must have been cold. I kept turning the photograph to the wall and my mother kept turning it back. You can still see the thumbtack holes.

There were days when I forgot how angry I was with my mother. She was good at thinking up things that were fun to do, like taking us to the breakwater to gather mussels. The breakwater stretched far out into the bay and, leaping from rock to rock, I felt fleet as a deer. The sound of the water rushing through the gaps

My mother's breast

Maria Petrucci, Mary Grand, Edward Norman, and
my mother in front of our Provincetown house, 1953

between boulders added to the feeling of risk. After lying on a rock
to renew her tan, my mother would climb down into the water
and pry mussels off the barnacle-covered boulders. At home she
scrubbed the shells, cooked the mussels with a little wine and, together with melted butter and garlic bread, that was supper.

She was having a good time introducing Edward Norman to
all her friends. They liked him and were probably glad that he
had money—his father had made millions as a founder of Sears
Roebuck. But her friends surely noticed how high-strung Edward
was. I overheard my mother telling a friend that he was wonderful
but "hypersensitive." That was a term she used for me, too. It felt
like a compliment. She said that Edward had once had a nervous
breakdown, but he had learned how to control his feelings. He
was recently divorced from a beautiful and brilliant woman named
Dorothy Norman (the woman who stole Alfred Stieglitz from
Georgia O'Keeffe). She was a photographer, a writer, and a patron
of the arts who was deeply involved in social causes. In late August, we drove to the other end of the Cape and stayed in Edward
Norman's large shingled "cottage" in Woods Hole. I loved being
in a place where everything was good quality and where nothing

was haphazard. My bedroom had twin beds with matching bedside tables, matching lamps, and matching bedspreads. The soft cotton towels had monograms. My mother never had anything that matched.

When my friend, Grania Gurievitch and her mother, Nemone Balfour, came to visit us in Provincetown, Grania and I went to the movies and saw Anna Magnani in *The Golden Coach*. Flagrantly sexual with her cleavage bared like a weapon, Magnani had just started singing in a sultry voice when the theater's door opened letting in unwanted daylight. My mother and Nemone marched down the aisle shouting, "Grania! Hayden! Come out immediately!" Heads turned. Crouching as low as possible so as not to disturb people in the seats behind us, we moved out into the aisle and followed our mothers onto the street. Full of rage and shame, I asked myself how could these women who slept with men who were not their husbands and didn't feel in the least guilty about it decide that an Anna Magnani film was unsuitable for us?

For her dancing party, Blair decorated our mother's upstairs room with fishnets. Fishnets were the rage in Provincetown's bohemia in the 1950s. Some people even wore pieces of fishnet on

Me and Grania on Constant Dickinson's boat,
Provincetown, 1953

Grania (in hat), Charlie Jencks, and
Mike Macdonald on the beach, 1954

their heads. For music, we had a stack of Arthur Murray's dance
records. Blair and I had been playing them and practicing dance
movements for days. Blair invited everyone from the Horseleech
Pond area and from Wellfleet and Provincetown as well. The only
friend my age was Grania. The trouble was that she was so good-
looking and could act so grown-up, that Charlie, Mike, and Reuel
danced with her but not with me. Maybe that was because Grania
knew how to dance and how to talk to boys. I didn't even know how
to do the fox-trot, and I never learned to follow. Halfway through
the party, Blair turned the lights down. Couples started necking.
Grania and I went downstairs to bed.

In July 1953, my father wrote to Gaga about the progress of the
custody fight:

> *The conference yesterday between Lybie, myself and our two
> attorneys was rather a disappointment to me, although my
> lawyer seems encouraged. . . . It's all very mysterious to me,
> and frankly Mougouch and I are thoroughly fed up with the
> whole business, and as far as I am concerned I'm going to put it
> completely out of my mind.*

He had already been through a nasty custody battle with my mother three years before. Then, as now, he grew tired of arguments and lawyers, and the whole process was irritating to Mougouch, who just wanted to get on with her life.

All summer I held out the hope that my mother would relent, and I would sail to Italy with my father and Mougouch and my four younger sisters. My mother didn't want to talk about it. When we did discuss it, my stomach churned, and my arms got tense as if I were about to hit somebody. I would go into my room and shut the door. The problem was that I did not want to appear at the Barnstable Court to choose between my parents. The possibility of going to Italy with my father began to seem like a dream—a dream that combined the comfort of being part of a family with the fear of being lonely and lost in a new home in an unknown land. For weeks, my mother had been telling me that I couldn't go to Europe, and I kept telling her that I did not want to go back to Mexico. She gave many reasons why I would be happier with her—places we would go, all the fun we would have. I was twelve years old. I acquiesced.

In late August, on our way to visit our father on the pond, I told Blair that I had given up. I had known for at least ten days that I wasn't going to Italy with my father, but I had not had the courage to tell him. Our mother dropped Blair and me at the top of the Turkey Houses driveway. As we walked down toward the pond, I realized that this was my last chance to say something. After a pond swim, we walked along the narrow deer path to our ocean beach. My father went first, then Blair. Scared of what I had to tell my father, I lagged behind. He had fought to keep me. I had betrayed his love. We walked through shrub oaks, past the bearberry-covered knoll where Blair and I used to practice handstands, then up past stunted pines to the top of the dune. There we paused to survey the beach and ocean far below.

My father went down first, following the diagonal path made by a summer's worth of footprints. He walked slowly, the way adults do. Blair and I waited until he reached the bottom so that we could run down with no one blocking our way. I asked Blair if she would tell our father that I had changed my mind. She agreed and then, with a few ballet-like leaps, she was on the beach. I stayed at the top of the dune wishing I could cease to exist. Usually I galloped down the dune, but not today. I could hardly breathe. My father walked almost to where the waves came up. Blair joined him. I sat close to the bottom of the dune pretending to be absorbed in sorting pebbles. Knees drawn up, the two of them faced the ocean. They were very still. After a while they stood and walked toward me. "Let's go back to the pond," Blair said. "The ocean is too rough to swim." She whispered to me that he was sad but not mad. My father said nothing. I wished the good-bye was over. I could not look him in the eyes. I would not be part of his family anymore. Already I had let them go.

The court case in Barnstable was dropped. I would not have to go there and tell the judge that I wanted to live with my father. It was not that I was choosing my mother. I was choosing not to choose.

What I never wanted to leave was the pond. People can come and go, but the pond is always there, always the same water, water that knows every part of me. It is intimate. It is mine. Stretching all the way from the lily pads right outside our porch to the hill beyond the far shore, the pond gives both a sense of possibility and a feeling of safety, a hunkering down, a permanence.

A few days later my mother told me that I was going to go to a wonderful co-educational boarding school in Lake Placid, New York. The pictures of North Country School in the brochure made it look like fun, but it seemed strange to me that after fighting for me to live with her, she was now sending me away. I tried not to mind. The one thing I was sure of was that I didn't want to live in Mexico.

Before she flew to Mexico, my mother put me on a night train to Lake Placid. When she tried to give me a hug, it was awkward because I was holding my suitcase. Anyway, I didn't want a hug. I wanted to climb the train's steps as soon as possible and find my berth. I wanted to get it over with. I had not been on a night train since she put Blair and me on a train to go to boarding school in Vermont. That was five years ago. This time I was alone. I didn't mind being alone. I was not scared, not really. I lay in my berth picturing my mother's face through the train's window when she waved good-bye. I remembered how my breath fogged up the glass so that I could hardly see her standing there getting smaller and smaller as the train pulled away.

Postscript

From the moment I landed at the North Country School in September 1953, my life stopped being haphazard. From then on it consisted of boarding school, Christmas and spring vacations with my mother in New York City and Mexico, a few trips to Europe with her and her new husband Edward Norman, and summer visits with my father in Italy or Cape Cod. The distance from my mother during the school year allowed me to find my own order. Slowly I invented a reasonably constant self. I lost weight. I felt valued. North County put the pieces back together. Even though I was dyslexic and had been to eight different schools before entering eighth grade, with a little tutoring and remedial reading, I caught up to my classmates.

For ninth grade, I was accepted by the Putney School in Vermont. The first two years were happy. I felt like a normal person, a person doing and feeling what everybody else was doing and feeling. I was popular. I had friends. Then in my junior year, a thick, dark, viscous fog closed in. Vacations lolling about in the Mexican sun at my mother's house were a reprieve from depression. Sun on my body made me feel whole. But if depression retreated, my anger came forward. My mother's outrageous selfishness continued to infuriate me. She would do things like promise to take us to Taxco or Puebla, and then, at the last minute, she would back out, saying that her back hurt, or some other fake excuse. I kept pushing away from her, reading or sulking in my room.

My squashed-down rage did not obliterate my fascination with my mother's beauty and power. I couldn't stop longing for her admiration. I tried to impress her by reading some of her books about ideas. During one vacation, she lent me a short book about Existentialism by Jean-Paul Sartre and after reading it, I decided that I must take charge of my own life. Boarding school and having two expatriate parents helped in my drive for independence. But, for all my newfound strength, I could not forestall depression.

In the spring of my junior year, my English teacher asked his students to write journals. Mine made him sleepless because it described how I felt when I was depressed. He also admired my writing. But it wasn't his admiration I coveted the most. It was my mother's, so I let her read the journal. It scared her, too. As a result, for my senior year, she removed me from Putney and took me to Paris, where I lived with her and went to an American school. For the first time and to my horror, I was given grades, and the students' grade average, listed according to academic performance, was posted on a bulletin board. I decided I must work hard and be at or near the top of this list, which got me into Radcliffe College.

After my sophomore year at Radcliffe, I returned to Paris and lived with a French family until, sick of still being hungry after each evening's stingy dinner, I rented an apartment in Montparnasse with my best Radcliffe friend, Anne Lindbergh. By December, Anne and I had both been dumped by our Cambridge and Oxford lovers, so she fled to her parents in Switzerland, and I fled to New York and transferred to Barnard College. By the time I graduated in 1966, I was married to a Guatemalan (he was born in Paris and raised in Locust Valley, New York), and I was the mother of a daughter and a son.

Being a wife and mother left no time for depression. I was determined to bring up my children in an entirely different way from the way my mother had brought me up. My husband, a writer and editor named Philip Herrera, and I lived comfortably on the Upper

East Side and sent our children to Brearley and Collegiate, both elite private schools. My children were the most important thing in my life, and I tried to give Margot and John unconditional love and to give them the kind of physical affection and intimacy that my mother had not given to me. Nevertheless, much of my mother's self-centeredness hung on inside me. I could be a neglectful and irresponsible parent. Oblivious to our offspring, Blair and I would sit in the Eighty-Fifth Street playground gossiping and soaking up sun with our skirts pulled up way above our knees. (Being attractive to men was all important, and a tan helped.) Another time, when Philip and I came home from a party, we found Margot and John in their footy pajamas sitting on the elevator bench and going up and down with the elevator man. Our babysitter, who lived downstairs, had gone home because we came home later than we had anticipated. I still feel guilty, and Margot has never forgotten.

In the early 1960s, I learned to type by writing children's books that were much too long to hold a five-year-old's attention. Philip read one of them, and said, "You are quite a little stylist." This was

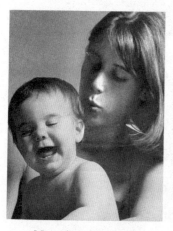

Me with my daughter,
Margot, 1962

Me and my son, John, 1963

momentous: Philip rarely gave compliments. When Margot and John were five and four, I wanted to understand what went on in their minds, so I took a job as an assistant kindergarten teacher. Once both children were in grade school, I decided that teaching art history to high school seniors would be more interesting. To that end, I got a PhD in art history. During my doctoral studies, I began writing for art magazines. My 1976 *Artforum* article about Frida Kahlo led to a commission from Harper & Row to write Kahlo's biography. This book also served as my dissertation. During research trips to Mexico, I based myself in Tepoztlán, living with my mother and her fifth and final husband, Peter Gerhard, a historical geographer twelve years younger than herself. (Her fourth husband, Edward Norman, had killed himself in 1955, leaving my mother with the Tepoztlán house and enough money to live for the rest of her life.)

My mother seemed content in Mexico until, at the age of seventy-six she became sick of its poverty—she grumbled about

My author photo on the book flap of
my Frida Kahlo biography, 1983

"open sewers," the inefficiency of help, and the lack of decent medical care. She sold her house and bought a house in Provence, where she built a small studio and painted every morning for the rest of her life. When I visited once or twice a year, our relationship improved. Her guest room had a desk, and I spent time writing at it. Wanting to be with me, she rattled around watering the flowerpots right outside my window. Now that she was old, she needed me more than I needed her. She wanted to know all about my life, and she was proud of my writing. She even read what I was working on while it was still on my computer. Finally, I had won her admiration. She cared. I wasn't mad at her anymore.

From this time on, it was my duty to make her happy. Maybe I had always wanted to make her happy, but now I felt guilty if I didn't. When she died in 1995 at the age of eighty-six, something enormous, like sunshine, like the pull of gravity, went out of my life. But only for a while: I can still see and feel the golden glow radiating from her formidable strength.

Both of my parents' fifth marriages were harmonious. My father, too, married someone much younger. Florence Hammond, the daughter of a Harvard classics professor, was twenty-eight years his junior and she gave my father his first son, Jonathan. My father stopped being an expatriate and bought a house in Cos Cob, Connecticut, where he resumed painting and printmaking and where he lived until his death in 2002 at the age of ninety-four.

After my biography of Frida Kahlo was published in 1983, I wrote monographs on the sculptor Mary Frank and the painter Joan Snyder. I followed up *Frida: A Biography of Frida Kahlo* with biographies of Matisse, Arshile Gorky, and Isamu Noguchi. I became involved with a group of feminist women artists and briefly participated in a feminist art journal called *Heresies*. The focus of my friendships and social life changed. Before, my friends had been Philip's Harvard classmates and their families. Now I turned more to the downtown art world. Perhaps in part because of the confidence that came with the success of my Kahlo biography, in 1984, I garnered the courage to leave my husband of twenty-three years. The four years that led up to that decision were blighted with depression. It lifted after I was divorced but did not go away forever. It returns every autumn and subsides every spring. For six months of the year I still fight it with antidepressants.

In 1988, I met and eventually married Desmond Heath, an English-born child and adolescent psychiatrist who had recently separated from his wife. Our marriage has been happy: we both love to clear land, build houses, and plant trees. Shaping land and houses makes us feel rooted in the earth.

Perhaps because our parents valued art and beauty beyond anything, all four Phillips sisters along with both of Gorky's daughters chose work that had something to do with art, and we all think we have a good eye for what is beautiful in art and nature. Indeed, one of our husbands called us "aesthetic fascists." Susanna Phillips and Maro Gorky became painters. When Blair married a second time to the painter Paul Resika, she took on the role of muse, model, and his most trusted critic. She organized her husband's exhibitions, designed his catalogs and posters, and created a splendid monograph on his painting. She is also a singer and an excellent photographer.

All the Phillips sisters spend summers on our father's pond. Blair and I share the so-called Turkey Houses and Antonia, Susannah, and our brother, Jonathan, share what was our father's and Florence's house, just a stone's throw away on the same pond. Blair and I used to feel cast out when our month on the pond was over and it was the other sister's turn to occupy the Turkey Houses, so both of us bought houses in North Truro. The fear of abandonment and loss that came with a childhood of being yanked from place to place and from school to school was assuaged by home ownership.

We filled our houses with things that we deemed beautiful. We are especially fond of chairs, wonderful shapes that, to us, are like miniature houses, very secure, very satisfying places to be. By owning houses, Blair and I have made our own permanent places, places that, when we are in them, leave no confusion about who we are or where we belong. No one can tear us away from our houses, no one can destroy the beauty of our worlds. For the last decade, Blair and I have lived in the same building on Manhattan's Riverside Drive. Her entrance is on the building's north side and mine is on the south. We don't even have to go outside when we want to visit each other and, when we look out of our windows, we see the same river.

The four Phillips sisters (me, Antonia, Susannah, Blair) with our father and brother, Jonathan, Cape Cod, 1992

Acknowledgments

My sister, Blair Resika, was and is a crucial part of my life and I thank her for helping me to travel back in time and for sharing the photographs that she took as a child. Blair's enthusiasm for my version of our story (often different from hers) has made the sometimes befuddling and other times painful pursuit of the past seem worthwhile.

Our childhood friend Penelope Jencks read my manuscript, added to my memories, and scanned innumerable photographs. I owe a debt of thanks to her. Penny Ferrer, always my favorite reader, went through many drafts. Her suggestions did much to shape and clarify my story. Mary Gordon, another wonderful reader, wrote notes on pages of the manuscript, each one insisting that I tell how I felt about things that happened. Rachel Urquhart, my daughter-in-law, read an early draft and gave me excellent ideas about structure and narrative flow. My son, John Herrera, had good ideas about building characters. His encouragement was important to me. Knowing how awkward it can be to read a parent's writings, I am deeply grateful for the generous help that my daughter, Margot Herrera, gave me. It was with trepidation that I gave her my memoir to read: Margot is a professional editor with a keen critical intelligence. While always kind, she can be fierce. And she is always right.

Many friends have shared their memories of childhood summers on Cape Cod and many sent me photographs to illustrate my text, among them Peter Chermayeff, Nicholas Macdonald, Reuel Wilson, Peter McMahon, Peter Matson, Kate Mannheim, and my cousins David and Barbara O'Neil. I also wish to thank Dean Rogers, special collection assistant at the Vassar College Libraries, for providing a photograph of Mary McCarthy and Edmund Wilson.

My thanks go also to Jeff Posternak, Mia Vitale, and Andrew Wylie of the Wylie Agency for believing in my book. At Simon & Schuster I am grateful to Priscilla Painton, Megan Hogan, Hana Park, Jessica Chin, and Patty Bashe for their diligence and help. Carly Loman's designs for the book's interior are just right and I thank her for that.

Finally, I wish to thank my husband, Desmond Heath, for his ideas and encouragement. Knowing that I had an insightful and willing reader by my side helped hugely in moving from draft to draft.

About the Author

Hayden Herrera is an art historian, critic, and biographer. Her doctoral dissertation about the Mexican artist Frida Kahlo became her first book: *Frida: A Biography of Frida Kahlo* (1983). Her other biographies include Pulitzer Prize nominee *Arshile Gorky: His Life and Work* and *Listening to Stone: The Art and Life of Isamu Noguchi*, which won the Los Angeles Times Book Prize for biography. To pursue her research for her Gorky biography Hayden was awarded a Guggenheim Fellowship. A Japan Foundation grant made it possible for her to travel to Japan to conduct interviews with people who knew Noguchi. Hayden has contributed articles and reviews to such publications as *Art in America*, *Art Forum*, and the *New York Times*. She has lectured widely, taught art history at the School of Visual Arts and at New York University, and curated several exhibitions, among them a show of Frida Kahlo's paintings that toured U.S. museums in 1978 and a traveling Kahlo centennial exhibition (cocurated with Elizabeth Carpenter) that opened at the Walker Art Center in 2008. Hayden earned her BA at Radcliffe and Barnard colleges and her PhD at the Graduate Center of the City University of New York. She lives with her husband, Desmond Heath, in New York City and Cape Cod.